life on a rocky farm

excelsior editions

AN IMPRINT OF STATE UNIVERSITY OF NEW YORK PRESS

life on a rocky farm

Rural Life near New York City
in the Late Nineteenth Century

LUCAS C. BARGER

transcribed and with an introduction by

PETER A. ROGERSON

Published by
STATE UNIVERSITY OF NEW YORK PRESS, ALBANY

© 2013 State University of New York

All rights reserved

Printed in the United States of America

EXCELSIOR EDITIONS
is an imprint of State University of New York Press

For information, contact State University of New York Press, Albany, NY
www.sunypress.edu

Production and book design, Laurie Searl
Marketing, Fran Keneston

Library of Congress Cataloging-in-Publication Data

Barger, Lucas C., 1867–1939.
Life on a rocky farm : rural life near New York City in the late nineteenth century /
Lucas C. Barger ; transcribed and with an introduction by Peter A. Rogerson.
p. cm.
ISBN 978-1-4384-4602-8 (pbk. : alk. paper)
1. Barger, Lucas C., 1867–1939.
2. Farm life—New York (State)—Putnam County—19th century.
3. Agriculture—New York (State)—Putnam County—19th century.
4. Country life—New York (State)—Putnam County—19th century.
5. Putnam County (N.Y.)—Social life and customs—19th century.
6. Putnam County (N.Y.)—Biography.
I. Rogerson, Peter. II. Title.

S521.5.N7B37 2013
635.09747'32—dc23

2012017668

10 9 8 7 6 5 4 3 2 1

CONTENTS

# FOREWORD BY THE AUTHOR

The author of this book was born and raised on a rocky New York State farm until his teens, and then went to the big city. But he returned at every opportunity to fish, hunt, and join in other country sports, thus keeping in touch with the changes of farm life as they came along. This is written as a variety book, of necessity, for the variety and kinds of work performed by the man on the rocky farm from the beginning have been greater than those of any other man under the sun, and it applies to the country woman as well. It is hoped that this work will appeal to the reader who does not like to read one subject so long that it becomes monotonous!

PREFACE

About ten years ago, as I delved into the history of my father's family, I came across a detailed and colorful description of rural life near New York City at the end of the nineteenth century. The manuscript was written in 1939 by Lucas Barger, a fourth cousin of my grandmother. It provides a lively account of farm life in Putnam Valley, New York, less than fifty miles from New York City. Because the version I saw was on microfilm and was not available locally, I had access to it for a limited amount of time. I glanced at it only briefly—but it was intriguing enough that I made a mental note to come back to it.

In the fall of 2010, I had an opportunity to visit the Putnam Valley Historical Society, which holds the typewritten version of the original manuscript. There I discovered two typewritten copies—one was the version typed by Lucas Barger's daughter Flossie, and the other was a version compiled and edited by Sadie Altman; she had come across the manuscript, found it fascinating, and took on the sizable task of typing it up. Altman noted that the manuscript was "divided into about 55 episodes, and covers the activities of a year." She also noted that "half of the episodes were published in the Community Current, a local Putnam Valley weekly newspaper. It was very well received at the time."

While at the historical society, I photographed each page of Flossie's typewritten manuscript, and the book I have put together here is based upon a retyping of that version. As I retyped it, I found myself captivated by Barger's vivid description of many facets of everyday life. Never before had I read a description of how eel racks were designed and used. I knew little about social customs at weddings and on Valentine's Day, and how very different they were from what we know today. As a geographer, I was fascinated by his astute observations on the natural history of bogs. I found each section not only enlightening but also entertaining. I developed an appreciation for not only Barger's knowledge, recollection, and ability to provide detail, but also for his folksy style, his anecdotes, and his wit. What makes this book special is the combination of Barger's knowledge of a wide variety of interesting aspects of farm life and his flair for writing.

The New York State Library has both the original handwritten version and one of Flossie's earlier drafts on microfilm. In addition, this microfilm contains copies of correspondence about the manuscript, consisting mostly of letters to Flossie from her father (these letters are also included in Altman's manuscript). The letters are fascinating in their revelation of how the two envisioned the project coming together. Lucas was clearly interested in publishing it, and he had sought information on copyright from Washington, DC, made an inquiry with a publisher, and entrusted Flossie with organizing the material and preparing it for publication. Lucas Barger died just one month after the last of these letters, in August of 1939. Despite the efforts of Flossie and Sadie Altman, the book never made it to print. In August of 2009 the work passed into the public domain, and I am absolutely thrilled to have the opportunity to, at long last, bring Barger's work to fruition.

I have made only a very small number of changes to the organization of the material. The section on "Maple Syrup" has been moved from the chapter on "Country Store and Election" to the chapter on "Incomes from Nature," and the section on "Snakes" has been moved from the chapter on "Country Store and Election" to the chapter on "Sports and Animals" (and the title of that chapter has been changed from its original "Sports.")

Included in the correspondence between the two are snippets of material on pigeons and bogs that are sufficiently substantial and interesting that I have added them to the main section of the book where these topics appear. I have also moved the chapters on "The Visit" and "The Quilting Frolic" to the appendix; they are not directly connected with the main text, but they do provide an interesting effort to capture elements of both local dialect and social interaction. I have taken the liberty of correcting the small number of obvious typos in Florrie's typewritten manuscript. In a few places, I have used square brackets either to make changes that make interpretation easier for the reader, or to indicate material that was unclear in the original. I have also added a small number of editor's notes to supplement some of Barger's descriptions.

—Peter Rogerson
February 2012

Acknowledgments

I would like to acknowledge the assistance of the Putnam Valley Historical Society and the helpful suggestions made by Sharmistha Bagchi-Sen, Joshua Clark, John Hudson, Christopher Rogerson, and two anonymous reviewers. My interactions with the people at SUNY Press have been nothing but positive, and I would like to thank Rafael Chaiken, Amanda Lanne, Fran Keneston, and Laurie Searl for their guidance, support, and assistance. Finally, copyediting a manuscript of this type requires extra care and expertise, and I am very grateful for the excellent job that Tim Loughman has done.

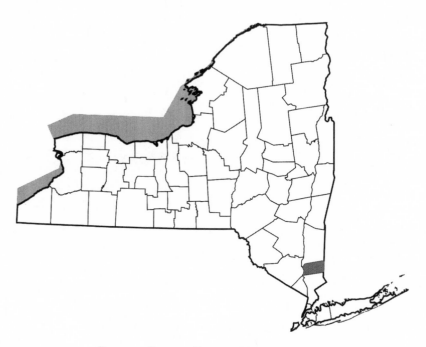

FIGURE 1. PUTNAM COUNTY, NEW YORK STATE

EDITOR'S INTRODUCTION

To fully appreciate Barger's highly informative and vivid description of farm life near New York City, it is helpful to place the work in context. His manuscript is ultimately a product of both the history of the region and his own background and interests. In this introduction, I first describe the history and character of the region, and then give some background on Barger and his family.

Putnam County, New York, lies within the New York City metropolitan area, at its northern edge. It is almost rectangular in shape, with its northern and southern borders lying about ten miles apart; each of these borders runs roughly east from the Hudson River for about twenty miles to the Connecticut state line. The New York counties of Dutchess and Westchester lie to the north, and south, respectively.

The population of the county was between 10,000 and 15,000 at the time of its establishment in 1812, and it remained virtually unchanged for well over a hundred years. Despite the fact that the county's southern border is less than forty miles from New York City, elements of geography and history acted in concert to impede urbanization and development until the 1930s. Dutch traders purchased these lands in 1691 from a group of native Americans known as the Wappingers; they in turn sold it to the Dutch American merchant Adolph Philipse in 1697. Philipse was granted a royal patent for these lands, which were also known as the South Precinct of what was then

Dutchess County. Beginning around 1740, the name was changed to the Fredericksburgh Precinct, and Philipse began to lease the land to tenant farmers. The feudal-like system he employed deterred settlement, and it continued after the patent had passed upon his death in 1749 first to his nephew Frederick, and then to a son and two daughters of Frederick, following Frederick's death in 1751.

In 1772, the precinct was subdivided, and the western portion (extending about eight to ten miles east from the Hudson River and comprising the present towns of Philipstown and Putnam Valley) became known as Philipse Precinct. It was not until the early 1780s that settlers could become landowners; it was at this time that the state's Committee on Forfeitures confiscated and sold at auction the land belonging to Frederick's two daughters, who, along with their husbands, had been loyal to the Crown.

In addition to the inhibiting effects of the land tenure system, settlement and growth were also impeded by the terrain. The Hudson Highlands rise more than 1500 feet above the Hudson River and sea level, and occupy the western part of the county. They were formed over a billion years ago by the collision of two protocontinents, an event that led to igneous intrusions and the formation of metamorphic rock such as the gneiss that is widespread in the area. The region is carved by several valleys running in a roughly north-south direction, and is bounded by steep slopes. Blake (1849) notes that "the mountainous and rocky surface of [Philipstown] will always present an impediment to an extended culture," and "there are few men of wealth here, but the inhabitants seem to be in possession of the necessities, if not the comforts of life." He goes on to say that Putnam Valley is "rough and mountainous," although he also points out that the Peekskill and Canopus Valley portions of the town are "rich, fertile, and well cultivated." A topographic map of the portion of Putnam Valley occupied by the Bargers clearly shows the rugged terrain. Elevations of around 300 feet along the Peekskill Hollow rapidly give way to elevations of around 1000 feet at the top of the aptly named Granite Mountain to the west and in areas not far from Barger Pond to the east. The cluster of households near Barger Pond lived on a small plateau at around 800 to 900 feet.

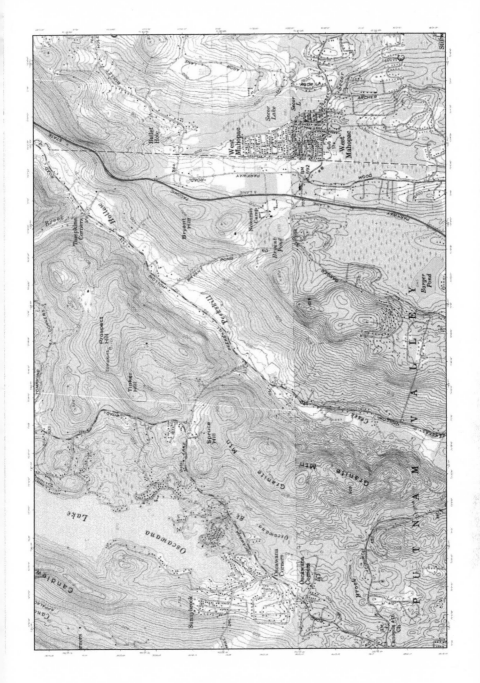

FIGURE 2. TOPOGRAPHIC MAP OF A PORTION OF PUTNAM VALLEY, NEW YORK

Source: Mytopo (www.mytopo.com). Used with permission.

As the population of New York City grew rapidly at the end of the nineteenth century, so too did that of Westchester County, immediately to the north. This was not the case further north in Putnam County, where both the terrain and the consequent lack of good transportation limited interaction with New York City. As industrialization and mechanization began to make it more difficult to earn a living from agriculture, Putnam County residents took in boarders from the city who were interested in spending all or part of their summers in the country. It was not until the 1930s, after roads had been paved during the Depression, and the Taconic Highway had been completed through the county, that rapid population growth began. The population of the county grew from 15,000 in 1930 to over 90,000 by 2000. It was precisely at the time when population growth began to increase rapidly that Lucas Barger set out to collect his thoughts and memories of life on the farm. He was witness to many of the changes that took place, and he describes in detail the variety of ways residents of the area found to make money, as well as the increasing difficulties they faced as the economy changed.

Lucas Crawford Barger was born in 1866, the youngest of four children born to Cornelius and Phoebe (Crawford) Barger. The two middle children died three years before Lucas was born, and Lucas grew up with the firstborn, Daniel, who was fourteen years his senior. Andreas, the progenitor of the Putnam Valley Bargers, was present among the early tenant farmers in the 1740s. Through Andreas's son John, who served in the Revolutionary War, the family produced a long line of farmers who remained in the immediate vicinity. Cornelius was John's great-grandson, making Lucas a member of Putnam Valley's sixth generation of Bargers. An idea of how prolific the family was at producing farmers is obtained from the 1870 census, which shows twenty-four Barger households residing in Putnam County. At least twenty of these were headed by farmers. (There was also one railroad conductor, one butcher, one "gentleman," and one whose occupation was not stated.) A map of Putnam Valley and Philipstown in 1868 shows the locations of at least fourteen Barger households in the small area near Lake Oscawana and Barger Pond. (The distance, "as the crow flies," between these two bodies of water is less than three miles.)

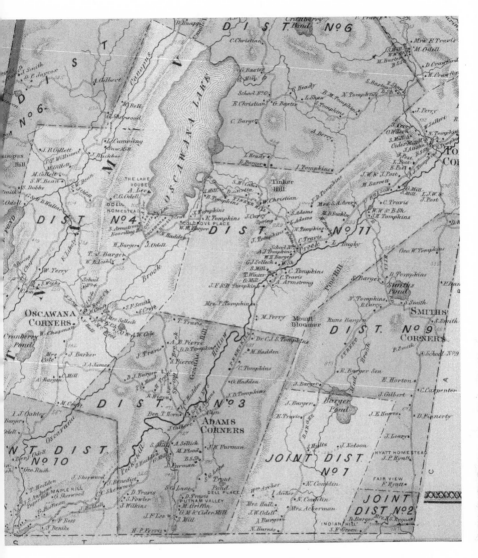

FIGURE 3. 1868 MAP OF A PORTION OF PUTNAM VALLEY.

Source: Beers, F.W. Towns of Putnam Valley and Philipstown, Putnam County, N.Y. (with) Carmel. Atlas of New York and Vicinity from Actual Surveys. 1868. Obtained through the David Rumsey Collection (www.davidrumsey.com). Used with permission.

The 1860 census reveals that, among the 285 households in Putnam Valley, the Tompkins (twenty households), the Odells (eighteen households), and the Bargers (fourteen households) had the largest presence; no other surname claimed more than six households. At its peak in 1870 and 1880, the Barger population of Putnam County numbered more than one hundred.

Records from the Non-Population Schedules of the 1870 Census permit a detailed look at Cornelius's farm. Ninety of the one hundred acres he owned were improved, and the family had two horses, four cows, and two oxen. They produced 25 bushels of rye, 50 bushels of corn, and 50 bushels of oats. Farm output also included 300 pounds of butter, 300 pounds of Irish potatoes, 12 tons of hay, and 60 dollars' worth of orchard products. Similar records from 1860 show that grandfather Daniel's farm was twice as large.

Lucas and his wife, Kate, born to Irish parents, were married in 1898. According to the 1900 census, they lived with their one-year-old son on West 20th Street in New York City, where Lucas was employed as a stationary engineer. In October of 1905, immediately following his mother's death at the beginning of the month, Lucas bought a farm near his old stomping grounds in the vicinity of Lake Oscawana. His father died in December of 1909, and the following year the family, which by then had grown to include two young daughters, moved back to New York City, where Lucas was employed as a steamfitter. By 1920, Lucas had moved the family to Peekskill, on the east bank of the Hudson, just south of the Putnam County border. At the time of his death in 1939, he was staying with his youngest daughter, Doris, and her family in Croton-on-Hudson, just south of Peekskill.

Barger had three patents in his name; these patents represent examples of his keen interest in detail. In May of 1899 he received a patent for a new means of sealing bottles. In July of the same year he received a patent for a venting faucet, and subsequent patents made by others for alternative venting faucets refer to Barger's design as the earliest in a sequence of patents. He received a third patent for a gun-sight design in 1901. With his agricultural pedigree, his penchant for details, and his flair for writing, Lucas Barger was well positioned to write an account of rural life in Putnam Valley at the turn of the century.

The letters to his older daughter, Flossie, show that the effort to put his writing together in the form of a book began in March of 1939. In May, he worried that his theme of illustrating how industry pushed farmers out of a livelihood might be problematic: "It maybe I hit big business hard enough to queer getting it printed. Many times that had an effect, and then again it may be a help, I don't know." In a letter the following week, he emphasized one of his primary goals for the beginning of the book: "I purposely did not go into much detail in the beginning because I don't think that would interest the general reader. The main thing I wanted to show was the way so many sources of income was taken away from the man on a rocky backwoods farm." In early June, he revealed some of his thoughts on style: "I read something along back, that a publisher wrote, and he said, 'Do not change your style.' He claimed the style was sometimes the best part. And I guess that is what you are getting at. If you can call my scribbling a style, and you think it 'odd' use it any way you like. For my main intentions were to write an odd book as I told you once before. The books of today have too much sameness. They appear to be written by the mile, and each one is a chunk cut off." Another letter to Flossie reiterates this, stating, "I would like to produce a book that is just as far from the general customs as possible, and get away with it. There is too much sameness to the books of the present day."

In some of the letters he adds additional detail to the material in the book, including mention of the fact that members of the Brooklyn Dodgers boarded at their house "in vacation time." He also occasionally adds some insight regarding the general state of affairs; for example, "It is true that there was plenty of ways of making money in Grandad's day. But it continued and improved for a little while after his death. Everything was going along good when I was ten years old (1876). But in a few years first one thing and then another petered out."

The combination of these firsthand observations on a dying way of life, together with his detailed descriptions of everything from barn dances to sowing grain, make this book informative, insightful, and enjoyable. With this long overdue publication, readers may take pleasure in the narrative, the anecdotes, and the fine points of farm life, and they may also be intrigued by this unique perspective on the changing cultural and socioeconomic aspects of rural life near New York City at a key point in the history of the region's development.

SOURCES

Beers, F.W. 1868. *Towns of Putnam Valley and Philipstown, Putnam County, N.Y. (with) Carmel.* Atlas of New York and Vicinity from Actual Surveys. Beers, Ellis, and Soule.

Blake, William J. 1849. *The history of Putnam County, N.Y. with an enumeration of its towns, villages, rivers, creeks, lakes, ponds, mountains, hills, and geological features, local traditions and short biographical sketches of early settlers, etc.* New York: Baker and Scribner.

Census of Population. 1860 and 1870. US Department of Commerce. Washington, DC.

Pelletreau, William S. 1886. *History of Putnam County, New York: With Biographical Sketches of its Prominent Men.* Philadelphia: W.W. Preston and Co.

Putnam County Historian (Brewster, NY). *A brief history of Putnam County.* Accessed online at http://web.archive.org/web/20080316122830/http://www.putnamcountyny.com/historian/

I

INTRODUCTION

According to what has been handed down, the farmers in the rocky sections of New York managed to get along fairly well for many years, after the trees were cleared from a section large enough to raise grain and garden truck, and also form a meadow and pasture section. The writer is quite familiar with what transpired on these farms back to the year 1876, and it is from that date on that mention will be made of these doings and things pertaining approximately to them—in my own way.

During a regular conversation, occasionally someone may say, "Let's change the subject," or, as is generally the case, it changes spontaneously. Then why should a book be expected to confine itself to one subject or line of thought until it becomes monotonous? If a variety of thoughts in a short space of time may come to your brain through your ears with agreeable effect, why can't a similar variety come through your eyes, as in reading a book? Anyhow, there won't be any chalk line walking in this.

Of course, there was no great quantity of grain raised, for the farmers were compelled to use oxen for plowing, and they were as slow as molasses. Horses were so speedy and jumpy that when the plow caught fast to an invisible rock, the plow was likely to break, or the plow handles might fly around and break the plowman's ribs, if he did not watch himself. And then again, he had to harvest his hay and grain with hand tools—the cradle and sickle, or reaper, for the grain, and the scythe for the hay. His threshing was all done by hand with the common staff and swingle (loosely tied together, and called a flail). Some, who had a semi-rocky farm, used a mowing machine drawn by horses on small patches, but in many cases the cutter bar had to be lifted over rocks so often that a large percentage of the grass was left on the ground. He depended as much, and sometimes more, for his cash income on other sources as on tilling the soil. Some took advantage of one thing, some another, as opportunity afforded, and didn't do badly at all. But all of a sudden, whatever the farmer turned his hand to that had a dollar in it was swept away from him, and with such regularity that it seemed as though a curse had been put on him.

Lost sales for many of his products, the coming of one pest after another that was unknown before—to eat up his garden truck and kill his trees, or give them a disease that made them worthless except for firewood—one machine after another, and chemical processes that supplanted his hand labor, and the quantity of natural food lost, and that was no small item; all this was the farmer's lot.

If history should repeat itself, and those old rocky farms get cleared off again, it will be about as much work as it was when the big primitive timber was on them. The trees are in greater number now, and in parts where the farms have been abandoned the longest, they are large also. On account of the cattle running on them, they became somewhat enriched, and this second growth grew faster.

They have a machine for pushing over and uprooting trees on the delta of the Rio Grande River. If there were one that would push the rocks and trees off together, it would be fine. If the rocks and trees would burn up together, it would be fine if another crop of rocks would not show up from below, but one always does. I guess the expansion of Hades forces them up. There are fields that have had the stones that could be lifted carted off every spring season, for as many years as the farm had been worked, generally several decades. If there were fewer of these backbreaking, scythe-dulling shin skinners the last year than the first, nobody could notice it.

One old guy said that, when the devil went out to sow the rocks over the face of the earth, he had them about half sown when he arrived in that section. His bag string broke and let the remainder all run out, and he went off and left them. Suppose there was war going on and the flying machines were dropping explosives on the cities and towns. Would not places like these backwoods farms be safest? The people would be so scattered that all they could kill at one time wouldn't pay for the ammunition.

Some say the "Hessians" drove the first settlers back in the rocky nooks, where they could elude their pursuers to better advantage. The fact remains, they went there for some reason, and it wasn't because of a shortage of good smooth land near the coast, for what few people there were at the time.

Perhaps they wanted seclusion. That seems to be the nature of some people. To this day, there are a few that prefer to live way back at the dead end of the road. Well, for that matter, we have some bon ton people in the city who like a penthouse! I can remember when some of my janitor friends were ashamed to say that they lived rent-free in a penthouse. My, how people do change! They used to want to live where they could see and hear all the hubbub of the street, and now they want to get away from it. Puts me in mind of that old saying, "It used to be the caper, but it don't go now." Those that like it can come as near to pulling the hole in after them in a penthouse as anywhere, though in some cases it might be well to keep a flying machine on the roof, in case of fire.

PEOPLE OF PUTNAM VALLEY

With regard to stock, they were mostly Holland Dutch, with a sprinkling of English, Irish, and Scotch, and practically no other races at all. I am of the four strains: Tompkins—English; Barger—Holland Dutch; Odell—Irish; Crawford—Scotch.

The first were Dutch weavers that went back in "the brush," and that is six generations ago. All of my forefathers from that day down were born in Putnam County (formerly Dutchess, and then Hoop-pole County). But I dare not let that out, for if you mention Putnam County, I may get my hair pulled out or get in jail.

Everybody is related that is of the old-time stock, be they Adamses, Lounsburrys, Duzenberrys, Nicholses, Christians, Currys, Baxters, Rundles, Travises, Purdys, Lees, Armstrongs, or a lot of others. They are like a lot of scabby sheep, all run out. So I don't see why they should expect much of me. I guess I better say nothing about the stock, for fear that I may put my foot in it.

EXODUS OF YOUTH
AS A CAUSE OF ABANDONED FARMS

Getting back to the rocky farm, the general procedure used to be that when the children came to the age of reason, they saw they were in wrong, and at the first opportunity dusted out into the outside world, and took what they could get, leaving the old folks to mourn, and scrabble along as best they could, with sometimes a little help and sometimes none, until they "passed out of the picture," and then there was another abandoned farm!

One of the fellows that made his escape from one of these farms and became rather prosperous, after being away twenty-five years, went back to look his old birthplace over. He could hardly recognize it. The forest trees were growing along with the apple trees in what used to be the orchard, and some of the forest trees were taller than the apple trees. And there were white birch trees some thirty feet high with the underbrush so thick that a rabbit couldn't get through without losing a lot of fur, growing where the corn and potatoes were growing when he went away. In the dooryard, the old lilac bush was alive yet, and trying to have some flowers on it, although fighting for its life in a jungle of young forest trees. The house had rotted beyond repair, as well as the barn and the granary. The old natural spring had so many alders and other small trees growing around it that he had trouble getting a drink. He said it made him feel sad.

He went from there to find some farmer that was still sticking it out to have a talk. He found out that at last something had turned up to help out a little. The farmers can now make a few dollars working on the roads and also by working for city people that bought some of the later abandoned farms, and fixed the buildings up before they were too far gone, so as to have a place to spend the summer. Now that the ice is broken, maybe something else will turn up to help out. When he got back to the city, in making fun of the place, he said he saw a chipmunk sitting on a rock trying to eat a gravel stone, and the tears were running down his cheeks. There isn't one chipmunk now where there used to be a dozen, so I don't believe they got much nutrient from gravel stones. When Darwin said, "the survival of the fittest," he should have said the survival of the well fed.

There was one of these farms within fifty miles of New York City as the crow flies that (before the cards were stacked against this rough country) raised seven boys to manhood. It consisted of 365 acres, with forty acres cleared of forest trees. It bordered the whole eastern shore of a lake that was an eighth of a mile long. It had a house that was plenty large for two small families, in fair repair, all ordinary outbuildings, a brook running through the yard, a natural spring, a good orchard—in fact, a place as good as any of the rocky farms, except that it was "back in." It sold "underneath the hammer" for nine hundred dollars around 1889. It cost more than twice that to put up the buildings. It was bought by a fellow that tried to get along by selling cordwood. And now the place, with a lot of adjoining farms, is a hunting and fishing preserve. And under the existing conditions that is all it is good for, and judging from the number of Indian arrow points that are found, they used it for that purpose aplenty.

And the rocks were a handicap to them as well as to the whites, for nearly all the arrow points found are broken, showing that about every time they shot an animal and missed, the point would strike a rock and break.

SUCCESSFUL FARMER ON SMOOTH FARM
IN ROCKY COUNTRY

There was a farmer that got him a little level pocket of about twenty acres in a valley with a brook running through it with lots of rocky territory around it. There are very few of these level places in these sections. And he paid, or agreed to pay, what was considered a very stiff price at that time.

He raised all the hay and grain he could on the level and stoneless part, and fed it in the wintertime to young stock that he had turned out in the summertime on the rocky part to shift for themselves.

Every spring he had a "vandue" (auction, to you) and sold off the older ones. He kept bringing them up from calves, and did this for some twenty years. He sent his boys to college, and retired with fifty thousand dollars. By wintering the stock in his barn, he had all the fertilizer for where he raised his grain and hay. A smooth farm in a rough country is worth much more than a smooth farm where everybody else has got one.

II

What Grandpop Said

My grandfather was nearly eighty years old when I was a boy just old enough to remember some things that he told me, some of which were being transacted almost a century and a quarter back from this year of our Lord 1939. He said all blacksmithing was done with charcoal until only a few years back, when they began to use soft coal, and the only kind that was any good was Cumberland coal. They made all their own horseshoes and ox claws from bar iron until a machine came out for stamping them out in several sizes with the gutter and nail holes all in, leaving nothing for the blacksmith to do but change their shape a little to comply with the variations of the different horses' and oxen's feet. Of course, the heels of the shoes had to be turned down and sharpened to keep them from slipping on the ice, and also there had to be a toe piece welded on each shoe, and they made all their own horseshoe nails out of "Swede's iron" that came over on a sailing ship, until they were made by machinery and it was cheaper to buy them than make them, unless the blacksmith had nothing else to do.

Axes were all made at the forge, until the machine-made ones appeared, and some blacksmiths forged out a rifle barrel and made a rifle on the plan of the "Kentucky" rifle.

The shad run up the small brooks from the rivers and the ocean to spawn, and by making a "scap" net one could get all that was wanted to eat fresh, or to salt down, as they did sometimes. A scap net is made by cutting and trimming a slim young hickory pole about one and one half inches in diameter at the butt; the pole is bent around at the tip and fastened to itself to leave an opening to fit the mouth of a large bag, or a bag net made out of horses' nets, which they used to use on horses that were going to funerals or some important affair. They were hung with fancy tassels. When these nets got a little worse for wear and became discolored, they made fine scap nets, after reshaping them.

They had "shin plasters" for money, five, ten, fifteen, twenty, twenty-five, and fifty cent bills, and at one time they had postage stamps for money. One of the farmers had a lot in his trousers pocket that he forgot about, and went out to plow on a hot day. The perspiration went through his pocket, and when he got back to the house, he happened to put his hand in his pocket, and it was one big gob. He soaked it in two or three changes of warm water, and finally diluted the "gum" of mucilage as it was called now, and by very careful manipulation got the stamps separated without tearing the paper, and took them to the bank, and they fixed it up so he did not lose anything. Very few farmers put money in the bank, for they were afraid of banks. They were "bustin' up" all the time. Their system of banking was to get their money in gold and silver in a shot bag and hide it in a stone wall, by taking a stone out and putting the bag behind it, and then putting the stone back, some dark night.

My grandfather said that when they first plowed a piece that had just had the timber cleared off it, they would find quite a few "Injin's arrers" on it, and now and then a white flint spear head eight or nine inches long, and very seldom a sky-blue stone hatchet, softer than flint, with a hole in it about an inch across and maybe five inches through the head of it, for the handle to go in. He had heard that the squaws made these holes by rubbing a stick between the palms of their hands, turning it first one way and then the other. By keeping sand and water under the end of the stick and a little downward pressure on it while they held it between their knees, they would finally get a hole through. There was rarely an arrow point found with a three-cornered point joined to the arrow point proper by a small neck, and no doubt this was used with poison on it, and was intended to break off in the wound. Apparently this kind of point was so delicate that it was rarely ever shot without its being broken off. He said the blue-black flint that most of the points were made of must have come from way off, for there was none around here. He was told the way they shaped their points was by heating them in the fire and then putting a drop of water from the end of a stick on the part that they wanted a small chip to fly off of.

Before stoves came around, they had nothing but fireplaces, with their old andirons, and the "swinging cranes" to hang the big iron dinner pots, and more recently a Dutch oven. Some of the houses were constructed so a horse could draw in the "back log" and then, after being unhitched from it, go right on through and out the other door. The intention of using this back log was to hold fire for several days, for if the fire ever got out, it was a case of running to the neighbor's to borrow fire, for probably the tinder was out, or there was nothing around to use with it that would flame from it. They had a way of wrapping live coals in something that would smolder for a long time, and when opened up, and blown on with the hand bellows, which every house had, it would flame up. Sometimes their calculation went astray, and when they got back home and opened up the wad, the fire would be out, and there was only one thing to do and that was to go back, and if the temperature was down around zero, as it was many a time, maybe the borrower's ears already frosted a little, it wasn't quite so nice. They neglected things the same as we do now.

The first things that come out that they called matches, they made themselves, pine sticks with one end dipped in "Brimstun." These brimstone matches would not strike, of course, but they would flame up with very little fire to get them started, and they made such a high heat that they would light most anything that was fairly good "kindling." He said none of the men folks ever wore drawers but sometimes they wore two pairs of pants in bitter cold weather, and sometimes the pants legs in the boot tops, which made a great difference in keeping the cold out.

Everybody did their own boot repairing. They used wooden lasts, and put soles on with a "peggin' awl" and sugar maple pegs. For years they made their own pegs, but soon they were machine made, and could be bought to better advantage. They had a boot rasp to rasp off the ends of the pegs, if they went through. The long "Brussels" from some big hog's back was saved for putting on the ends of a waxed end, which is quite a little trick in itself. In sewing up a seam, or on a patch, the two ends are put through past each other, the bristles being passed through first from opposite sides to get a start, the hole being made first with either a straight or a crooked sewing awl, the crooked one being used for putting on a patch. The ends being drawn from both ways made a very durable stitch. Some made their own shoemakers wax by boiling down pine tar, but it soon became so cheap, that was a waste of time.

When boots were needed, they were made by a traveling cobbler. He came through with a kit of tools half as big as a horse ought to draw. Sometimes, of course, he would get a lift. He took the measure and made the boots right there, charging a certain sum, with his board thrown in. He had his own leather along, and things he called his "trees," and that is what he shaped the boots with. There were three sizes of these, and they could be adjusted to let one size start in where the others let off. When the factory boots came out, these cobblers were out of a job, except for a few who got a job in a factory.

This is the way we used to take the measure for boots: When the heel touches the baseboard, make a mark on the floor half an inch in front of the big toe. Mark each side of the foot on the floor. Make a stick half an inch longer than the foot is wide. Then make one equal in length to the distance from the mark in front of the big toe to the baseboard, and get boots that these sticks will just fit in. See that there is normal toe room up and down, and they will fit whomever you got them for when you get home. If there is pressure on top of the toes, there will be ingrown toenails. We never wore any shoes until a few years back, and then we liked "gaiters," for there were no shoestrings nor buttons to bother with. Pull 'em on, and you were done till you pulled them off. Pull 'em off, and you were done till you pulled them on. But the rubber on the sides soon lost its pull, and the tops would gape open and look sloppy, and they would feel like they were going to fall off your feet when you walked.

There was an outside stone oven for every few families, where they would bring their bread dough in baskets and bake it, and someone would get up early and have the oven hot when they came. When the oven got hot enough for the soot to take fire, and the fire commenced to crawl around without flame, that was the sign that the oven was hot enough, and all the ashes and what lighted coals were left from the wood were pulled out with a hoe, and the bread was put in with a long-handled flat wooden shovel to bake. Their Johnny cake, or corn bread, short cake, and "sweet cake" were baked in a Dutch oven at their fireplace after the Dutch oven came, but before that by a reflecting oven, and potatoes were sometimes baked in hot ashes and coals, a piece of light tin being used as a reflector, and were pretty good, except for the raw and burnt portions.

Before the Chinese dishes, called "china ware," came over and reached the backwoods, all they had were tin dishes, and "pewter platters" to bake pies in. The pewter platters would sometimes get overheated and melt, and they would have to be mended by a tinker who traveled from house to house, the same as the cobbler did. He had molds with him that he could cast entire platters with, and he had "dams" that he could attach so as to patch a platter by getting the platter almost to the melting point before pouring the patch piece, everything being heated by a charcoal fire.

Before the iron pipe came along, galvanized inside, what little pipe was used was lead, it being used to lead water to the house where the spring was above the house. (Galvanized pipe was made a long time before they found out a way to galvanize the inside where there was no light.) These old tinkers knew how to wipe a lead joint, and could make all repairs. Not so long back, the hydraulic ram came out, and lead pipe was used nearly always for that, but by that time the old tinkers were off the job. The glazed earthenware, sheet iron bake tins, and the China dishes took away their jobs.

Stoves came along and everything was baked in tinware, or glazed earthen platters, and if a hole got in a tin they would pull a rag in it, and get along with it until they could solder it, as most of them had learned to do, and tin soon became so cheap it was best to throw those with holes away.

One big boy nearly lost his life by a rag that was drawn in a hole in a pan. He would go up in the garret and pour a little powder out of the rock powder keg and bring it outside the house, and with a long iron rod, one end of which they had heated, they would touch the powder off. The rag got afire and wasn't noticed. When he went to put some more powder in out of the keg, he went through the roof and up in the air. He lived, and that was about all.

The fall-sown rye would be up four or five inches high in the spring as soon as the snow was gone, and there were so many flocks of wild geese going north at that time, they were a pest, for they would alight on the green rye and eat it. They would bite it off close to the ground, doing it mostly in the night. Sometimes, half a dozen flocks would be in the ryefield in one night, and where every flock had been, the next morning there would be a spot eaten off forty or fifty feet across. Sometimes, when they were heard babbling, someone would take the old musket that was loaded with buckshot, and sneak up as close as possible, and fire in the direction of the noise. Now and then, if he was lucky, there might be a dead goose or more lying in the field, in the morning, and they had goose to eat. If any was killed out of a flock, that flock would go on north, and nearly every flock would go on north after one night's feeding. But there were some flocks that would stick around several days, going to lakes in the daytime, and back on the rye again at night. Sometimes they would alight on the rye in the daytime, but were easily scared off. In fact, they were so wild that it was hard to get within shooting distance of them. The rye that they had bitten off would grow up again, but would be way behind the rest, and when the rest of the field was fit to cradle, that would still have milk in the grains, and would shrivel when it got dry. And if the cradle was kept out of the whole field, waiting for the part the geese had gotten to to get ripe, then the rest would be overripe, and a lot would fall out of the heads and be lost when it was harvested.

The wild pigeons used to roost in the tall bushes between the edges of big timber and a bog swamp, and we used to take an old lantern that could be darkened, or partly darkened, as we liked, by slipping it under our coat, or a bag. One fellow had a bag slung on his shoulder, and another handled the light, as many of these pigeons could be reached from the ground. The light thrown on them wasn't more than enough to see them distinctly, but was enough to dazzle their eyes. They were grabbed quickly and quietly, across the butt of their wings, to keep them from fluttering and making a noise, or the whole flock would go pitching and diving off in every direction and spoil everything. As soon as one was caught, the fellow who caught it would either bite its neck or wring it, and after waiting long enough for it to become so near lifeless as to be beyond fluttering, it was dropped in the bag. My grandfather said they could most always get all they wanted in a couple of hours, maybe half an oats bagful.

When they went spearing pickerel along the edge of the lake, they had a light that gave aplenty. It was used for no other purpose, and was called a "jack light." It was made by a blacksmith, and was an iron basket on a long rod. This so-called basket had four times as much opening between what might be iron splints as the width of the splints themselves, and plenty of light could get through. White birch bark was burned in these baskets. They used homemade scows, or skiffs, sometimes made from the trunk of a tree, but rarely. The "jack staff" was stuck down in a hole in an iron basket strongly fastened to the side of the boat, near the stern. It was put at an angle so that the basket would be out over the water far enough to keep the sparks from falling on the spearer's head, but not so far as to be out of reach for adding birch bark to the fire when needed. The fellow with the oars backed the boat slowly along, quite close to the shore, the distance varying according to instructions from the spearer. The spear had a flat part on the handle, so the spearer could always tell the position of the tines without looking at it, and would know from the sense of feel how to turn it quickly so as to have the row of tines crosswise of a fish, no matter what position he was in. (It was all pickerel, suckers, eels, and some large yellow perch that were speared in those days. Black bass and white perch were not in the lakes then.) The spears were generally seven tined, and were always made by the local blacksmith. Wherever there was an outlet from a lake, in the fall of the year, and sometimes as early as the latter end of August if there were heavy rains, the eels would go down these outlets by the bushel, and on some of these outlets they used to put an "eel rack," made of slats with openings between them for the water to run out, but not the eels. This box or rack was generally about four feet square for a small stream, but larger for a larger one, for it had to let the water out through the slats as fast as it came in, or the box would fill up and overflow, and the eels would go with it. The box was so arranged that all the water of the brook could be led by a wooden sluice over the top of it, and allowed to fall into it, and the sluice was so arranged that a gate would turn all the water out of the sluice and make it go on past. The bottom of the rack was just a little higher than the brook proper, so it would become empty as soon as the sluice water was shut off, giving a chance to get the eels out. It required at least a seven-foot fall, but ten was better, With a lesser fall, the rack would have lower sides, but needed a greater floor surface and longer timbers. When the eels saw that they were caught, they would try to run back up the stream. On a fair-sized stream from the first of September to the fifteenth of October, a bushel of eels in one night was an average catch. When there were big rains, some streams that flowed strong enough to fill about a thirty-inch pipe yielded two barrels.

Some old-time cider mills were made by making a circular wooden trough sixteen inches wide, the circle being twenty-five feet in diameter. This trough was made by framing out and joining heavy timbers, making the joints neat as when building a boat, and the seams of the trough were caulked the same. The adz was used to make the trough. This trough had to be on a solid foundation and fixed so it could not move. A section of a large tree trunk was set about ten feet deep into a hole in the ground in the center of the circle, leaving about seven feet of it projecting above the ground, and stones of all suitable sizes were jammed around it to keep it solidly in place. A large roundpin was inserted through a hole bored crosswise through the butt end of a second trunk—a long, slim one tapering from about ten inches in diameter to six—and then into a hole in the top of the trunk projecting from the ground. This lateral trunk was carefully rounded where it crossed over the trough and passed through a wooden wheel twelve feet in diameter, with a face to fit in the trough. Apples were poured into the trough from barrels or bags. Oxen were yoked to the outer end of the axle stick, and as they walked in a circle, the face of the wheel crushed the apples. Once a considerable amount of cider and crushed apples had been produced, the dipping began with a wooden dipper into wooden pails, the cider being strained out into barrels, and the crushed apple portion dumped into the old wooden screw cider press. Neither the cider nor the crushed apples were ever allowed to touch metal of any kind, as it made poor cider, and sometimes made it black. When the mill started, everybody had their job, and it was a continuous performance—one driving the oxen, one putting the apples in, one shoveling crushed apples out of the trough with a wooden scoop, sometimes two dipping out juice (keeping out of the oxen's way), and one standing by at the press until he got enough for a "cheese," when he commenced to screw down the press. One cheese is all they crushed apples for at one time, as a rule, unless there were two presses. They sometimes used a storage for crushed apples, but it takes about twelve hours to get the cider practically out of the cheese, and it is not good practice to keep the crushed apples around too long before putting them under the press. The storage becomes sour unless there is a lot of labor put in it, but when the cider is going to be converted into vinegar, the storage can be used to advantage, to the extent of one extra cheese that will be put on the press in about half a day. Each bushel of apples yields four gallons of juice, that taken from golden russets late in the fall, just before freezing weather sets in, being the best.

III

Handcrafts—

Ways of Making Money

SHIP TIMBER

The earliest income to be derived from a source that did not interfere seriously with the regular routine of farming was from the production of ship timber.

A small percentage was procured from white oak, but the main supply was chestnut. There were stern knees, keels, bow pieces, and what not. It was necessary for some parts to be cut from a sizable tree, for they squared up sixteen by eighteen inches. A tree with a large limb forming an almost right angle with the body brought the highest price, because this shape could always be converted into a stern piece that formed part of the keel, and furnished a solid upright portion for the rudder attachment.

Some of the white oak pieces were fifty feet long, and their removal to a vessel from far back in the interior—uphill and down, over very poor and narrow dirt roads—was an impressive undertaking, and cost plenty. Added to transportation was the initial price of labor for scoring with the common axe and hewing with the broad axe. Consequently, it was an expensive consignment of timber that reached the seashore.

The day came all too soon when the farmer fell out of step with the early "march of progress," for steel supplanted timber, and in a surprisingly short time.

CORDWOOD

No doubt there has been more profit realized from the sale of cordwood than from any other sideline pursued by the farmer. Gradually, however, this commodity has become of less importance. The introduction of coal and oil stoves, the consumption of coal in place of wood in brick kilns, and the limited use of wood in the manufacture of charcoal have combined to make its market value negligible.

Cordwood is never used for a farmer's firewood. At schools and churches it is, because it can be measured and is not so unsightly as sled-length wood. Hickory is never cut for cordwood except on special order for smoking meat, and sells for at least twice as much.

Hardwood is all the farmer used in wintertime, and in summer dried-out softer wood for a flash fire that soon died out after a meal had been cooked. On bake days, dry hardwood is used.

If cordwood was used at the door, there would be a lot of lost labor. However, city people who live in the country for the summer buy cordwood because it can be measured.

RAILROAD TIES

Next to cordwood, railroad ties brought in the best returns. In fact, it was customary for the farmer to obtain the two products from the same trees. After the ties were removed, the remainder of the wood was cut into cordwood lengths. There was a sparing amount of oak used for this purpose, but nearly all was chestnut. Well, the chestnut blight blighted this enterprise, good and proper! There was not enough oak to make profitable its exclusive use, and oak was much more difficult to score and hew.

The railroad officials recognized the need for a substitute and adapted southern pine, dipped in creosote. The faces of these pine ties did not present the smooth, attractive appearance insisted upon in the purchase of their northern predecessors. A young Rocky farmer summed up his impression: "Puts me in mind o' my Pop's head when I first set to cut his hair." (For many years, the members of one family, or a group of neighbors, depended upon reciprocal service in the art of barbering. Some became very "handy" and were in demand, especially among the more youthful swains. Beginners often left their subjects in a state of doubtful elegance, however, for the results of their efforts were highly irregular.)

TANBARK

The peeling of white oak and hemlock for tanbark was a money-making operation during the latter half of the nineteenth century. The performance entailed a seasonal difficulty, since the peeling had to be done in the spring of the year (when the bark would slip), and this interrupted plowing.

A generation earlier, sumac leaves were picked in huge quantities for use in tanning and dyeing. Whole families, including the children, engaged in this activity. It was not considered dangerous, since the leaves did not scratch, nor otherwise injure the skin.

Sumac was used for tanning and dyeing, and it was used for the higher class of tanning calfskin high-topped boots, called dancing pumps, and also calfskin gloves.

Chemists eventually produced a fluid called tannin, and this virtually disposed of the demand for bark. Similarly, a cheaper substitute had long since replaced the use of the sumac leaves.

HANDLES

Our northern shatterbark second-growth hickory is coarse-grained and not particularly pleasing to the eye, but it is the toughest and most durable wood in America from which to make handles for such implements as the adz, sledgehammer, pick, pitchfork, hoe, rake, and many others.

The southern hickory is whiter, with an almost imperceptible grain. Handles made from it are prettier to look at, and will, for this reason, outsell the northern variety.

An expert of former days could fashion an axe handle with an axe, and finish off with a jackknife (until the spoke shave arrived). The smoothing process was accomplished by glass and sandpaper.

After a few dollars were picked up making handles by hand, the irresistible power of the Machine Age asserted itself once more, and out came what they called an "ober lathe,"* which riddled out all kinds of handles like lightning. This discovery made possible the production of all kinds of handles at a comparatively lightning speed, and that was that for handmade handles.

THE AXE

There is one thing sure: if those old farms are ever cleared off again, the axe will have to fly. As man hewed his way up from the wilderness, the axe was the most efficient tool ever given to him. It is wonderful what a great variety of useful things an expert can make and do with it. He can rough out ox yokes, sled caps, sled shoes, and benches, almost complete the handle for the axe itself, sharpen bean poles and fence stakes, shape sled stakes, and make wooden wedges and dozens of other things, besides putting it to its main use, that of getting timber and firewood. He takes as good care of the head of his axe as he does of the blade, because he uses it for driving pins, wedges, and many other things. He never allows it to hit, or be hit with anything harder than the iron itself. In years past, there was many a wooden plow made with it, though that will probably never be done again. Today the axe is mostly used to cut firewood, and this firewood proposition is a bad one. There is more labor performed in proportion to what good is got out of it than with any other work on the farm. First, it is cut in sled lengths in the woods and dragged to favorable points in heaps, where there is a fair chance of being able to get the old wood-shod sled near it without breaking the oxen's or horses' legs in the rocks, and for the most part in recent years it has had to be drawn on bare ground. Snow, of course, is a big help. Then it is piled up at the house. The next operation is to cut it into short stove lengths, splitting it down to proper

---

*George Ober received seven patents for lathes and lathe improvements between 1865 and 1897, and in 1891 the Ober Lathe Co. in Chagrin Falls, Ohio was formed.

size. Then it is ranked in the wood house, if there is one; if not, it is left where it is cut, out in the weather. Then it is carried by the armful as wanted, and lastly the old woman gets her fingers full of splinters chucking it in the stove, and she has to watch the fire almost all the time to keep it doing what she wants it to, and then sometimes makes a slip. If the cake she's baking goes flat, then she and the old man have it out about the wood being too wet or something. Oh, well, that is a pretty good time to go out and attend to some of those chores!

Working with an axe is a backbreaker the same as practically everything that is done on a rough farm, only more so. A man cuts wood more with his back than he does with his hands and arms, and his back is the first to tire out. It isn't everybody that can afford a power saw or to pay someone to come and cut his wood. The man who can't has to labor at a disadvantage to get a few cents.

A man ought not to be more than a yard tall with long arms to work these farms, so as to be right down on his job. How many things can you think of in the way of work that he doesn't have to bend his back at? The axe, the cradle, the scythe, the sickle or reaper; planting potatoes, hoeing potatoes, digging potatoes. Planting corn, hoeing corn, planting the garden, seeding the garden, hoeing the garden, picking beans, etc. Pulling up the various things that grow in the ground, binding the sheaves of grain in the field, ditching, cutting bogs, working the road, picking up apples and nuts (when there are any). Making hay, threshing with a flail. But what is the use—I could keep on for a mile yet.

The Society for the Prevention of Cruelty to Animals should prevent the preacher from expecting one of these farmers to bend over in church, where he finds the only time he gets to straighten up.

BASKETS

By dressing out rectangular strips of black ash wood and pounding them carefully with a hammer (the face edges of which had been rounded off), the grain could be made to separate without injury to the wood. The resultant nice white strips were the "splints" from which all sizes of first-class baskets formerly were made. Peck-and-a-half bushel baskets with bow handles and bushel corn baskets with "ears" or separate handles were the most common.

One old basket maker remarked optimistically, "They can't make a machine for makin' baskets anymore'n they kin fly." He felt secure in his little business, but with relentless certainty there soon appeared a machine for making baskets, and another for making splints. Not content with thus destroying the old basket maker's complacency, inventive genius actually made it possible for him to see men fly!

The machine-made baskets were not so good for durability, but they were good enough to replace the custom-made articles. In the eyes of big business they were much better, for they would last about one quarter as long, and four could be sold during the life of a single handmade basket.

HOOP POLES

There were four sizes of hoop poles that brought an appreciable gain to the farmer—those used for flour barrels, tights, tierces, and hogsheads. The only kinds of wood employed were young white oak and hickory.

The tidy sum of one hundred to five hundred dollars was pocketed by many an industrious man engaged in this trade every fall and winter. Some split the poles with a one-hand adz and, with the aid of a drawing knife and shaving horse, prepared them for the cooper's use. This procedure was of double benefit to the farmer, for he realized much more on the sale of the poles and saved on the expense of shipment. Alas for ingenuity! Along came iron hoops, steel hoops, flat hoops, and round hoops, climaxed by noncorrosive, flame-resisting galvanized hoops. The farmer had to shift his cud and think up another way to make a dollar, for his hoop pole business was gone!

CHARCOAL

This was burned, or rather semiburned, in a heap shaped like a haystack in what was called a coal pit, although it was above ground on a level spot. The first section of cordwood standing on end was some fifteen feet in diameter, and the next section on top of this was smaller, and the next one smaller yet, and so on, until the structure came to a blunt point at the top. There was always a hole left in the center from the ground up for the purpose of airing it from the top after the whole structure had been covered in a thick coating of moist dirt, packed down hard, and sometimes sod, the object being to keep it nearly air tight so as to support only partial combustion until the process was finished. It had to be watched day and night, for if a hole opened up in the covering and too much air got in, the whole thing would burn to ashes, and after getting much of a start, the fire could not be put out with the crude facilities at hand and only one man on the job. It paid to keep awake.

It had an agreeable odor and could be smelled a quarter mile away, and if they were moving the finished product and the wind was blowing in the right direction, you didn't have to get much nearer than that to get all black. Nowadays, it is burned in a closed tank, in town, and steam blown through it at the right time to glaze it, and it can be handled with the fingers without getting them black. Plumbers and other mechanics use blowtorches in place of it now a good bit. What money it used to bring to the backwoods is gone forever, and what they used to get for the creosote that they drew out of the pit near the bottom with a pipe has gone with it.

THE SQUAW MAN

There was a man from this rocky section who went out west, stayed a few years, and married a squaw. When he came back, he brought her with him. He used to burn and peddle charcoal for a living. He had a poor old pair of horses and a rickety old secondhand wagon, with the regular-sized charcoal body on it. The bottom of it had been patched and repatched. He and his wife and their three children went to town with a load of charcoal to peddle out. After they sold it all from door to door (the people then used it to start fires and were not so particular as they are now), they got a bottle of rum, put the children down in the deep wagon coal box, and started for home. As they had about nine miles to go on a hilly dirt road, and the old plug horses were slow, by the time they got to within three or four miles of their old hut they were both drunk, both being only sober enough to get the horses unhitched, and crawl in their old bed, which was on the floor. It was two straw mattresses placed side by side, so they touched one another, and made one bed for all. When they woke up late next morning, one of the children was missing. The man went down the road about two miles and found him at a store, where somebody had brought him, having found him groveling in the dirt in the middle of the road and not known what it was until he got out of his wagon ahead of the horse. The child, of course, was as black as ink, just as everybody is who is around charcoal. He had simply fallen through the bottom of the old patched coal body, and they never missed him. These children, when they were from ten to twelve years old, used to go out of their old shack and slide across a frozen-over mud puddle in front of the door, and then slide back and zip back into the shack again. They were barefoot. The thermometer was down around zero, and they were frozen like the Bible says Eve was.

The squaw used to take a four-barrel salt sack, and cut a round hole in the middle of the bottom, and then cut a little off the corners. She stuck her head up out of the round hole, and her arms up out of the corners, and she was dressed! That was the poor thing's everyday suit. She had an old dress that she went to town in, but whatever color it had been, the charcoal made it black. When the children got big enough, they left, never to be heard from again. When her man died and left her alone, she went to work for a farmer and, becoming sick of life, took Paris Green shortly after it had come around to kill potato bugs with. She had learned to talk a little of the white man's language, and just before she died she said, "Ah, me make mistake"—whatever she meant.

IV

Incomes Directly From Nature

FURS

Up to about thirty-five years ago, there was some money in trapping, and the buyers came through and paid cash, so a fellow knew where he stood. But there have been so many stumbling blocks put in the way—posted lands, so many dogs, traps, license tags, a sprinkling of city people who used to kick because the farmers posted their lands, and then posted theirs as soon as they got possession, etc.—that there is not much in it anymore, and no buyer comes through, for there isn't enough fur caught to make it worth his while. At present, there are a few farmers, or their boys, who skin a few furs and send them away and then get skinned themselves. There was an exception to the above during the World War, when the price of fur went sky high and then dropped back again.

A steel trap being a cruel way to make a dollar, that is one lost income that a good many don't grieve about. Some day they may find a painless way of killing animals. Let us hope so.

NUTS

The passing of the chestnut was a calamity, felt by young and old. It was the main dependence of many a poor boy as a means of getting his winter boots and maybe an overcoat, for they were always saleable. Everybody liked chestnuts! Well, that damnable blight made a clean sweep, and defied mankind to do anything about it. Once in a while, a chestnut used to have a round hole through the shell, and there would always be a worm inside. And the boys would sometimes say, "Well, there is one nut they can't get into, and that is a hickory nut!,"—which was a poor prophecy. Not many years after, there was some kind of a pest that stung the young hickory nut when it was a tiny, soft thing, pod and all, and lo and behold, when the nut came to maturity, so did a big fat worm that had eaten more than half of the meat, or kernel. Probably ten percent or more of hickories are in this condition now, and as the trees bear very poor lately, there is not much in shattering hickory nuts anymore, or white walnuts, as they are sometimes called.

In the olden times, I have known a farmer who had a lot of trees standing out in open pasture land, where the cattle helped to enrich the land, to gather forty bushels, and he got four dollars a bushel for them. Black walnut and butternut trees bear next to nothing nowadays. The black walnuts have a split-pit disease—the two halves of the nut are separated or gaping open in places. And what few butternuts there are, are false. The trees of both used to be loaded down, and with sound nuts, too.

ROOTS AND HERBS

Sometimes there would be patches of boneset, or of motherwort, of a quarter of an acre or so, that had very little other stuff growing with it, to be sorted out, and could be mowed and handled the same as hay. These patches paid some. And the leaves and blossoms of peppermint dried in the shade were worth gathering, until they cultivated forms of it in Michigan and the price went flop.* White root and

---

*Editor's note: At the turn of the century, 90% of the world's supply of mint oil came from within a ninety-mile radius of Kalamazoo. Source: "Mint in Michigan," by Leroy Barnett. Department of Natural Resources, State of Michigan. http://www.michigan.gov/dnr/0,1607,7-153-54463_18670_18793-53363--,00.html

white snake root soon got dug out to a "fare thee well," and there was only one root left that had any real money in it, and that was "ginshang," as we called it, its real name being ginseng, which means "man root" in the Chinese language. There were fellows from the Bowery in New York that the farmers dubbed "professional diggers," who used to beat their way to Canada and start digging about the first of August, and live off the country by begging and otherwise, all the way back to the city. They generally could sell what they dug to a dealer in the city for enough to live on in one of the cheap hotels on the Bowery until another season. I saw one of these fellows about fifty miles from the city on his way in, and he had a carpet bag over half full, and as ginseng was worth seven dollars a pound at that time, he probably got one hundred and fifty dollars for what he had. This root around the time of the World War got to be worth twenty-three dollars a pound, and there was such a scrabble for it that one might as well prospect for gold nuggets as ginseng roots. It is ridiculous what they want to pay for common medicine roots and herbs and what they sell them for in some cases. I bought a little package of catnip for a lady's cat at a drugstore in New York for ten cents. I weighed it, and there was less than half an ounce. That meant that it retailed for three dollars and twenty cents a pound. I have at my elbow right now a list of prices paid for herbs and roots by a dealer, and catnip is listed at four cents a pound, and the seller must pay the parcel post charges. Bloodroot is listed at four cents a pound. Let anyone dig enough of this root to weigh a pound when it is dry, and see how much labor is involved. It should be worth at least a dollar a pound, and this is only one of a whole list that they buy for practically nothing. Do the savages somewhere dig roots for brass buttons? A fellow digging medicinal roots at the prevailing prices would have to be at it a long time before he could retire from business, if he retires on more than fifty cents.

BEES

"Yonder comes Hiram aleggin' it as tight as he kin. Wonder what in Sam Hill's the matter? The steers an' the plow is standin' stiddy anuff." She opens the door and she is greeted with "Hey, Hanner, grab the tin pans and the dinner horn quick! Don't you see the bees a-swarmin'?" They get where the bees are in a jiffy. He being pretty much out of breath takes the pans, and she the horns, and bedlam breaks loose. The bees that are fixing to go away are all up in the air getting their traveling formation perfected. The noise prevents the bees from hearing the queen's orders, and after a while she alights on some nearby tree branch or bush, and the bees all alight with her, forming a bunch that is the shape of a pineapple with its bottom end up, but the size of a water pail or thereabouts. Once they alight, they never go away until the next fair day, if unmolested. After they have all settled down in a bunch, Hiram goes back to his plowing and she gets some hickory leaves, makes a little salt brine, and with the leaves rubs the brine all over the inside of the spare hive (called a skip by the farmers). The brine will be dried by evening, leaving a thin coating of salt scented with the hickory leaves, and the bees seem to like this. Then she gets a bed sheet and has it ready. In the evening there are two fence rails or poles laid parallel about fourteen inches apart, and the sheet laid across them, leaving a deep sag in the sheet between the rails. Just before dark, the limb that holds the bees is sawed off without doing any shaking, and the swarm is carried carefully to the sheet on the rails. One person holds the skip with the edge of it on a rail, but tipped over almost at a right angle to it. Now the one who has the bees on the branch places the bees closely over the slack part of the sheet that will be under the skip in a second and gives the limb a quick, short jerk that lands the bees down in the pocket, and the skip is rocked over with its other edge resting on the other rail, so quickly that the bees have no time to do anything about it. About once in a blue moon the queen bee is killed this way by being crushed between the rail and the edge of the skip, and if so it is just too bad, for all the bees die off. After the hive or skip is turned over them, the bees are left alone for an hour or two to give them time to crawl inside. It is then taken and set where it is to remain permanently. The next fair morning, the bees will come out, and circle around, and probably keep it up more or less for half a day, and then settle down to business.

Some claim that when bees swarm they will come out and light on something nearby without making any noise. If anyone wants to lose all their swarms, let them try that. It has never happened where I come from.

If anyone wants to get some bees gratis, let him fix an empty hive as explained above, and set it in a favorable place early in the spring, and later on there will be a swarm in it. Don't make the mistake of setting mockernut or pignut leaves instead of shatterbark hickory. That from young trees is best.

There are always swarms getting away from someone, and occasionally they swarm with wild bees out of hollow trees. The advance guards that pick out a place to go when they swarm are more likely to choose your empty hive scented to suit than a hollow tree in the woods.

HONEY FROM BEES

Up to about fifty years ago, bees did well. Many swarms would average fifty pounds of honey the first season. That made from buckwheat was of a strong flavor, which most people didn't like, but a few would have no other kind. That made from basswood and white wood sold the best. People used to kill the swarms at the end of the season if they wanted their honey. The "patent hives"—those having little boxes in the top of the hive, to let the bees steal out and live, and winter on the honey they had left—were known, but not used. The bees were stricken with cholera from some kind of poison flowers one season, and although their hives were well filled, every last one died off as soon as they commenced to eat their stores, and bees have never amounted to much since.* They were German, or little gray bees, and were supposed to be unable to get the nectar out of red clover and several

---

*Editor's note: During the fall of 1868 and the following winter, there was a massive die-off of bees in the United States. Bees died in record numbers of dysentery; the disease was called "bee cholera." Problems persisted with the disease across a wide range of the country for a number of years.

blossoms on account of their proboscis being too short. But the Italian bees that took their place with their longer proboscis have never half equaled the German bees' honey harvest in general. The poisoned honey tasted fine. No one could detect any queer flavor, but those who ate it almost died from what appeared to be cholera. It even affected the hogs that ate it. No one dared sell it, and several of the farmers lost at least two hundred dollars that year. To say nothing about their loss in future years. I was present when the trouble first was discovered. We dug a little hole in the ground, and stuck in the bottom a split stick that had a rag in the split that had been daubed in melted sulfur, and after picking out a hive that appeared to be heavier than the rest, we took it to the hole, set fire to the sulfured rag, and set the hive over it, banking the dirt around the bottom to keep the sulfur fumes in. After a time, we pounded the sides of the hive lightly to jar the dead bees from the hole, as was the custom. But lo and behold! When we showed the lantern light in the hole, there wasn't a bee in it. They must have all flown out and died in the open, nor did we find any in the hive. The honey was weighed, and there was sixty pounds, hive and all being weighed first, and the weight of the empty hive deducted after the honey was out. So there was no guesswork. Wild bees seem to do the same as they have always done, and they always were conundrums. When you cut a bee tree, you never know whether you are going to get enough honey to eat on one short cake, or a couple of wash boilers full. However, the latter seldom occurs. Everything considered, in the eastern states honey as a money getter is a thing of the past.

SHEEP

There is no better moneymaker on the side than sheep, and there is no better place than New York State to raise them, for they do well here. But there are two *ifs* connected with the business. One is practically a prohibitive one, and that is dogs. Once one or more sheep are killed by dogs, and the rest harassed, the survivors of the flock never do well. The other *if* is fencing, and to fence a farm, with, say, a Page fence* would probably cost more than the farm did. Sheep are sure hard to keep in. They will go through a hole in a brush fence, and leave a lot of wool on the brush. And there is only one thing that can beat them going over a high stone wall, and that is a flying machine. A sheep-killing dog will dig under a fence that he cannot get through or over, and some dogs—generally shepherds—that take care of sheep at home will sometimes go ten miles or more at night and kill somebody else's sheep. It has come to a clash many times by the owners of both—"Which shall it be, dogs or sheep?"—and the dogs have always won out. Some who were lucky have done well with sheep for a couple of years, and then the dogs got in, and "Good night."

It seems to me that no matter how brainy a man is, he is generally a fool about his dog. If he has one that either kills sheep, sucks eggs, or bites someone now and then, it makes no difference to him. His affection for that dog is just the same, and he will always be telling about the great intelligence the dog has shown, that to an outsider sounds silly. Probably the door was open, and the dog came in out of the rain some time.

The town paying for the sheep that the dogs kill is a farce. If the town paid the market price for the whole flock and took away those that weren't killed to do what they liked with, maybe donate to hospitals or the poor house, there would be some justice in the town's ruling. Or another way would be to pay full price for the dead, and half price for the living, and let the farmer keep them. And even then the farmer would not be ahead any, for a flock once harassed by dogs are not worth half what they were when in a healthy condition.

TURKEYS

The old hen turkeys used to steal their nests away over back of yonder somewheres, and by and by came draggling along anywhere

---

*Editor's note: J. Wallace Page invented the first woven wire fence. Founded as the Page Woven Wire Fence Company in 1885, the Page Fence Company was incorporated in 1889, leading Adrian, Michigan to become the "fence capital of the world."

from ten to fifteen young ones. A few exceptions, of course, when a fox, the crows, or some variant had found the nest and cleaned it out. Outside of one the horse stepped on, one that the old sow got that was too careless around the hog trough, and one that got run over in the road, and maybe one or two other minor casualties—such as one a chicken hawk got before the old gun got him—they all grew up vigorous and healthy. After thirty or forty of them (which was about all a small farm could handle as a sideline) were stuffed with ground flint corn and loppered milk, they brought in a nice penny around Thanksgiving. And at Christmas, a late brood was sometimes marketed from the second nesting of a hen that had her nest broken up the first time.

Try raising them now! Many years ago, there came a disease they call "black head" that kills them off when they get a little larger than quails. The germ it is claimed is in the soil. If so, the germs must live a long while, for turkey raising has been tried on ground that has not had turkeys on it for twenty-five years previous, and they died just the same. A very few are being raised by keeping them off the ground, and great care exerted to keep them from contamination. After the fracas is over, there is not much profit from raising turkeys that way. There is too much labor involved. The good old easy way of raising turkeys is apparently gone forever on these rocky farms, unless some antidote is discovered for this awful disease.

Instead of the farmer taking a load of turkeys to town for Thanksgiving, he has to go there to get one for himself. Pretty tough, to have to eat a bird from Texas or some of the southern states, when he used to produce some of the best turkeys that ever flopped a wing.

CHICKENS

It is enough to give a fellow the gaps, when he thinks about chickens, for that is what more than half of the young ones used to die of. There was some money in eggs and chickens a part of the time in the past. But sometimes eggs got down as low as ten cents a dozen, and dressed laying hens to twelve cents a pound, and they are the best flavored fowl on the yard for fricasseeing, though they require more cooking than younger fowls. There is nothing in hens at the present time for the farmer, except to keep a small flock so as to have one now and then for his table, and for the eggs required by his family. A small flock gets a good part of their living picking around the place, and are not as apt to get the croup, or some other disease. Those who make a specialty of the chicken and egg business with a large number of fowls, and are located near the market, and are where they can buy their feed handy and cheaply by getting large quantities at a time, have the upper hand of the farmer that lives way back in, maybe on a mountainous dirt road. I will say right here that one of the worst features of backwoods farming is that the farm produces a little of many things, and not much of anything, and it makes the output hard to market, unless a private trade is drummed up in town, and then the storekeepers want to kill the farmer for not letting his goods go through the proper channels, even though at the time the stores may be glutted with the kinds of goods he wants to sell. And again, if he trusts his private customers, he will never collect from some. The fellow that has a regular chicken plant is not making any too much money, everything considered. He has a seven-day job, and has to keep his eye on the gun all the time, and while he has a big turnover, he doesn't have so much left. While I am writing about fowls, probably it is best to mention ducks as being no good on a backwoods farm. I have heard a farmer say that "he would just as soon try to fatten a fanning mill by putting grain through it, as a duck."

FRUITS AND VEGETABLES

There is a gum disease that attacks plums, cherries and peaches, and there is no preventative. It causes split pits and a deposit of a gum at the peach pit. The plum trees have chunks of gum on the body that have oozed out through the bark, and the green plums have little drops of gum sticking to them that have come through the skin, and they begin to drop off the tree before they are half green. The egg plum being an exception, as it is full-sized when it drops. None of our native plums comes to maturity anymore.

The old-fashioned sour red plums that made such fine preserves are quite a loss. Except in isolated places, there aren't any peaches to even have gummy pits, for the yellow leaf blight has killed all the trees, in spite of spraying. Apple quinces that used to grow so smooth and clear meated, now grow (when there are any at all) into a knurly lump that appears to have been stung a great many times by some kind of a devil bug. Anyhow, they are worthless, though some people try to make preserves out of them, bugs and all.

And citron! Another fruit, or vegetable (as you like), that made such fine preserves, some of which were dried and used to make fruit cake and mince pies, is practically a thing of the past. It rarely grows well anymore. This native citron of ours outranks the Italian citron about a mile. I never see any in market any more. Some try to imitate citron by using watermelon rind, but it is a sick imitation. There is no citron flavor to a melon rind, at all. It is flavorless, or very nearly so.

Our citron used to command a good price in market. The soil seems to have lost an element that citron needs, and also pumpkins. There are no deep-wrinkled, hard navel orange-colored pumpkins now. The kind that used to make such good pies! At present, they are pale yellow, almost as smooth as a football, and shaped like one. The meat is soft and spongy, and is what the "punk" pies are made of today.

Apples can still be produced, in a handicapped way, and are as good-flavored as those that grow anywhere, though they do not look as good as those from some other places. The trees all grow too much top for the roots to support, and must be trimmed back. The tops and inner limbs must be cut away to let the sun in to color the fruit, and by thinning this way, the tree spreads sideways instead of up in the air. Next, there is poison to buy, and a contraption to use with it, and a lot of labor lost using it. Such actions never were necessary in the olden times. They first began to use poisons when they discovered that Paris Green would kill the Colorado potato bug, or beetle, that came east in such hordes and, after eating all the potato tops, ate up the tomato vines. Some apples, such as Northern Spies, have taken a notion to decay with a soft and disgusting rot, right on the trees, before they have grown into full size. The best way to trim a tree like that is right to the ground. If apples grow in clusters, pick off enough of the little ones to give the others a chance, and do it early, before those cast away have absorbed such vitality from the tree. If the orchard is fenced in with a hog-tight fence, and the hogs turned in it, it will help the trees, and the hogs too. But do not expect to make as much out of apples as formerly.

VINEGAR

It used to be the caper to turn a lot of cider into vinegar, and get twenty-five or thirty cents a gallon for it. And, when juice was only worth four cents a gallon at the cider mill, it paid to get whiskey and other barrels, and go to it! A row of barrels out of doors, with a bottle stuck neck down in the bungholes, and a little "mother" (a slimy substance taken from some strong barrels of vinegar) put in each barrel to give it a start. Well, the "Winegar Works," as one old farmer called it, put the kibosh on that. They make vinegar now that is a total stranger to the apple. It smarts if it gets on the back of your hand. It has a nasty raw taste, and the fumes from it will eat a brick wall and crumble it off, and I have seen where they had to chisel off the crumbling surface down to the solid brick, and paint the wall with an acidproof paint. The question arises: if it will eat a brick wall, do you suppose it is good medicine for the wall of a man's stomach?

The chowchow and pickles that are put up in it, or vinegar that has been adulterated with it, is no good to me, nor to many others that used to be chowchow hounds. They will tell you that the sour part of the vinegar is sulfuric acid, no matter how it is made. Admitted! But—there is more than one kind of sulfuric acid, the same as there is more than one kind of alcohol. Rye alcohol makes rye whiskey, and wood alcohol makes death, for it is very poisonous. Still, it is all alcohol! This so-called synthetic vinegar is charged with sulfuric acid that is derived from a much cheaper source than from aging apple juice, and it has some ingredient in it that is a misfit in vinegar. But as long as it does the farmer out of a few dollars, everybody ought to be satisfied. He was only made to be kicked around, anyhow.

DRIED APPLES

There was an old lady who dried eighty dollars' worth of apples one winter in the kitchen, on shelves arranged high above the kitchen range, and as they were not dried out in the sun, and where there were no flies, wasps, nor yellow jackets, they were almost white. And she got twice as much for them as for those that were dried out of doors on flat rocks in the fall of the year, and were of a dirty, yellowish brown color. Several women got to doing this, and then, as usual, some inventor got wise to what was needed, and produced an "evaporator" that dried not only apples, but any old kinds of fruit, vegetables, or what have you! The old apple-peeling machine was thrown up in the garret to rust out.

MAPLE SYRUP

Maple sugar was of minor importance, with not trees enough to pay for an evaporator, etc., such as one finds in Vermont. Some make it for themselves, some sell a few dollars' worth, cutting wood, lugging sap, getting the kitchen all steamed up, with all the kitchen stove's limited capacity. This put it in the catchpenny class.

Sometimes a bunch of young fellows would come out from town and boil sap where some good-natured farmer would let them tap all the maple trees they wanted to. Some brought a tent, but a tent wasn't the thing, for the weather is pretty cold during the sap-running season and freezes at night sometimes. Those that built a lean-to and made the same fire to heat it that boiled the sap got along much more comfortably. They used to take away a lot of syrup that they sugared off on the stove when they got home, or maybe used as is on pancakes. When it is boiled down enough, it will form solid cakes when poured into paddy pans or the like, but if it is stirred continuously when cooling, it will be the same texture as light-brown cane sugar, and look like it. It is handier to have it in this form if it is to be put into cakes, or drinks also. A little can be used for flavoring better when it is in this form.

They thought they had a lot of fun, but there was a lot of hard work to cut wood enough to keep the old iron furnace kettle boiling night and day, out in the open, and there was a little fire on the side lit a good part of the time to cook on, and it was quite a chore to bring water from some natural spring that maybe wasn't too handy.

OTHER INCOME—SUMMER BOARDERS

Up to the time Saratoga, Newport, and a few other places of that kind opened up, there were a few dollars to be made boarding people, but it soon got so that many farmers would take what few they could accommodate at a very low price, just to get hold of a little loose money, and it ruined those that were trying to make a regular business of it. About all the good there was in the whole business was that their city cousins livened up the country when they were there, and for many of us, what glorious days they were! Some of us made friends that we mingled with in the city in after years. We used to make as much fuss and preparation to go to New York as we would now to go to Europe.

I made an elderly friend in 1888 who told me that the grandest time to live in New York City that he ever knew of was in the fifties. He said there were lots of people who retired on fifty thousand dollars, and that it was a common sight to see a retired gentleman and a small businessman, or maybe just a common laborer, talking to each other, without knowing or caring what the other's finances were. Everybody was neighborly, and nearly everybody was honest. But the millionaire and the semi-millionaire came along and spoiled it all. He said, "It seems to me that man is only on the threshold of civilization, and that retiring on fifty thousand dollars was a great step toward it, and that the millionaire system is a greater step from it." I for one do not want a million, nor even enough to be called rich. I may have trouble enough getting by hereafter without having to go "through the eye of a needle."

V

Life of the
Rocky Farm Women

GRIDDLECAKES, ETC.

The old man is plowin' over acrost the brook, but his mind is only partly on the old oxen and the plow. He is saying to himself:

"Hanner hain't got t' wash t'day, an' I hope she slips out and gits a mess of greens, yaller dock an' poke weed, half an' haf. If she goes over in the edge of the woods where the leaves is deep, I seen some poke there t'other day that had long white shanks, jes' like sparry grass, that growed up through them. She put a ham bone in the cellar t'other day, that had a lot o'meat on the shank that she sed was goin' to cook with a mess—mebbe she will! Jeslikisnot, she'll go up on the side hill an' see if there is enny o' them honey comb mushrooms (morries) under that old dead apple tree. It's time o' year fer 'em. I got quite a passel there last yeeur. If she gits anuff wuth while, and throws 'em in salt and water t'nite, they'll be fine fer brekfust. She tole me that she wasn't going' t'weed the unions t'mar mornin' till after brekfust, and she gathered up the hen zeegs. I kindly got a hankerin' sumhow, 'bout that ham bone! I hope she ain't bothered with that caff gettin' in the cowcumber patch agin'!"

The making of griddlecakes (called pancakes now) was done altogether different. They didn't believe in mixing up a batch of

37

batter, and starting right in cooking griddlecakes. They claimed they were unhealthy. Their cakes had to be raised, and after the raising was once started there was some batter taken out, and fresh ingredients put in, so the batter kept on raising all winter. They never believed in eating buckwheat in the summertime. It was marvelous to see the dexterity of some of the women around the kitchen. They never had a pancake turner till some time in the eighties, and used nothing but a common table knife. There was some of them could turn three large pancakes that had run and cooked together, all at one flop, and the whole thing would land within a whisker of where it had been, end for end, and bottom side up. The knife was got under after everything was loosened, about one quarter the way from the end, and the whole business was brought up with a swing that was enough to scare the cat out of the kitchen. It looked as though the pancakes were going to land all over the place.

Then she would run in the cellar and get a little pitcher full of milk, that was poured out of an eight-quart pan without spilling a drop, to come and thin the batter down. The stream was at least eight inches wide where it came over the edge of the pan, and the mouth of the pitcher was no more than three. The stream would get to be almost round away down below the pan, and that was where the pitcher was held until the pan was tipped back, and the last end of the stream was in the pitcher.

The old-time women did a lot of scientific work, as well as hard work, that the outside world knew little about, and it never will, because they are not only gone, but most of the things performed by hand are now done by machinery or a substitute that is near enough to pass. That mixing machine the automobile has made the city people more or less acquainted with the country, and also made the country man more or less acquainted with the city, but they have changed to a great extent, the country far more than the city. In fact, it is hardly to be called country any more. It is but a rural district. It was a common thing for the women to milk the cows, feed the pigs and chickens, maybe get fodder for the cattle, lead the horse to drink, and then bring in an armful of wood when passing the wood pile. These women didn't grumble like the city people do, at least not as much in the average, and good health and ruggedness must have been the reason. But don't think that when these women were doing outside work that the men weren't doing much harder, for they were.

There were very many women's jobs that came along and lasted for a short season, such as picking the live geese, tending the smoke-house with hickory chips after the hams were hung, spring house cleaning, preserving and canning stretched out over a longer period, riddling g——, I mean intestines, to get the fat off at hog killing time, generally with the help of a neighboring woman or two (the male neighbors helping with the butchering), making head cheese, stuffing mattresses with feathers, not forgetting the trundle bed that the children slept in, and was shoved under the big bed in daytime. There were new ticks to make now and then, and if the ticking was sent for, and the old man brought home a kind that they told him was 'just as good' at the store, then the fur would fly, and he would have to take it back, for there was only one kind of ticking made at that time that would not let the feathers work through.

The leaf fat of the hogs had to be cut up in small pieces, and tried out on the stove, an iron kettlefull at a time, that might take a week or so (this was true leaf lard). The souce had to be cleaned, which is the snout, the ears, the tail, and the feet. Some of the feet were cooked until the meat was falling off the bones. This meat along with the rest of the souce, and the meat off the hog's head (called preacher's face) as well as the meat from the lower jaw called the jowls, was made into headcheese. Except maybe one or two preachers' faces would be eaten at the table, as is, after being cooked.

And then, oh, gosh, the sausage! It was chop, chop with nothing but an old single-bladed chopper, every chance there was for over a week. Then the two-bladed chopper came out, which helped a lot, but when the sausage grinder came out that would really work, there was more fuss than when America was discovered. The sausage was seasoned with sage, or other herbs, and malt, and stuffed in bags about three inches in diameter and a foot or two long, that were made of some clean old linen cloth, like sheets that were getting weak, and were hung up in the garret to age, and be used as wanted.

Then there had to be about half a barrel of brine made of ashton salt, that would float an egg, or a potato. The upper head of the barrel had cleats nailed across it to hold it in one piece, and it was trimmed down around the edge so it could go inside the barrel. A handle was put on it, and flat stones laid on each side of the handle that were not quite heavy enough to sink it (this being a man's job). Then it was up to the women to pick "cowcumbers" as they got of suitable size, a few each morning, and put them in the brine with the floating lid on top of them, for they must always be kept under the brine, same as salted mackerel, or they will spoil, the same as the mackerel will. This was kept up until the barrel was full. They rarely ever bothered with the little pickles like your pinky, which were merely scalded in sweetened and spiced vinegar, and put in big-mouthed bottles. Around one and a half inches in diameter and five to six inches long was the size desired, and of a variety that had rather a smooth skin. There was a long, slim, very green kind that had more warts on it than a toad, that was not very popular except for its color. If the little cucumbers are kept picked off as fast as they come on, a vine that will produce maybe fifty of them, probably would only produce ten that are allowed to grow to the large pickle size.

FOODS

Now that you have read the dark, or hard luck side, pertaining to the rocky farm, it is proper that the other side should be mentioned, when such farms were in prosperous condition. We will consider food first. The rich people of the cities think they eat the best food that can be, or has been produced. But they don't. There were dozens of articles that were far superior to those on the market, or in the kitchen today, and this is based on firsthand experience in both city and country. Take butter, for instance. The butter that was made about six weeks from the time the new grass showed up in the spring, from Jersey cows, and made by the few real butter makers, had a most exquisite flavor, and a beautiful color, and has never been anywhere near equaled by the creamery process. And mind, if the liquid portion (called the whey) was well worked out of it, it could be packed in glazed earthen crocks, and kept for a year, if need be, in a common dirt cellar. Five-pound crocks were used for this, so as not to have too much exposed at one time.

Hams, nowadays, are salted a little, smoked a little, and away they go to market. It takes sixteen weeks to properly cure hams, eight weeks in what is known as a sugar cure pickle, which really has no sugar in it at all, but does have open kettle molasses as one of its ingredients. The hams were taken out and put back once every day, to insure all surfaces of the meat got the proper contact with the pickle. Then the flesh part was well rubbed with an equal mixture of red, white, and black pepper, and they were hung up and smoked another eight weeks, over second-growth green hickory chips—the young hickory having more of a gummy sap in it, and the burning of this sap gives the flavor, not the wood. Then if the hams were from preferably Chester white hogs, that were fatted on spring water and flint corn (no other food being used) and kept in a rather small pen to keep them from running their fat off, you had a superior article, and one the world knew little about. This flint corn makes the hardest fat of any food known. In the olden times, a bushel of it could be exchanged for a bushel and a half of the western dent corn at any feed store. But it was found that it did not pay.

The best beef that has ever been is produced by fattening up quickly an old farrow cow that is as poor as wood when you start in, by feeding her cut-up pumpkins and flint corn meal. Even the black Angus steer beef is not excepted. The Jersey and the Alderny cows excel for this purpose. Soft corn makes soft fat in beef or pork, and it cooks all to grease.

The potpie, the mince pie, the boiled black cherry pudding, the boiled huckleberry pudding, the boiled apple dumpling, are all lost arts. There is a thing they bake in an oven, nowadays, and call it an apple dumpling, that will give a pig the dyspepsia, and is enough to make some of the old-time cooks turn over in their graves. How they can call anything a dumpling that is not dumped in a pot, is beyond me. Bakeling, or bakething, would be more appropriate.

Of course, there are many kinds of food, such as pork cake, fruit cake, many kinds of preserves, mince pies, pumpkin pies, boiled apple dumplings and the various boiled puddings, that could not be made now of the same quality unless the lost ingredients could be reproduced.

Who would like to make the only real sauce that belongs on them? The body of which is, a pound of butter, a pound of real cream, and a pound of sugar, mixed, and melted together, and then nutmeg, vanilla, or some other flavoring added. When butter was sixteen cents a pound, the farmers didn't mind a little thing like that. It could be flavored with maple sugar, if desired, and a part of the farmers boiled out their own from the sap of their own trees.

(They say we do not know what we eat nowadays. Well, I have had a pretty good hint several times. To mention one, first there was a piece of apple skin, then a part of a core got stuck between my teeth, along came an apple seed, and at last I got a stem. That gave me a hint there were some worms in those apples, they never bothered to take them out.)

WOMEN FISHING

Yes, sometimes the women would break away and go fishing, and the lakes were so full of pan fish in the seventies that one of them could catch fish faster than a big boy could clean them—yellow perch, catfish, large-sized sunfish, and sometimes an old "golwallopin'" big pickerel. All were caught while standing on a rock on shore. When the six-quart pail was full of cleaned fish, the hike was started back home. The fish were lightly salted, and put down in the spring in a crock, and the lid was put on till morning. Taking care to let no water get in the crock. When fish are cleaned as soon as they are caught, and handled this way, they harden up during the night, and make altogether better eating. The spring water was cold enough to harden butter, and many a time it was kept there, for many farmers had no ice, and that was their refrigerator, even for meat temporarily.

MAKING BREAD

The making of bread was no small chore. There was a pot of "emptins" made with flour, and milk or water, that had some home-made yeast added. This was put back of the stove against the chimney in a warm place on a bench or chair at night, and in the morning some of it had probably run over the top of the pot into a milk pan that the pot was in. This was mixed with a lot more dough, and put in a large wooded bread tray, and put back in the chimney corner again, with a cloth over it, and it was called the "sponge." It would swell up to twice or more of its original size. Then chunks were cut out large enough to make loaves, more flour added, and some mashed boiled potatoes, then it was knead, knead, knead, until whoever did it was, or should have been tired out, when it was put in the oven and baked. When it came out, that which was to be kept was sprinkled with cold water when hot, wrapped up in a clean linen cloth, and put in one or more of the glazed crocks, and a lid of some of the same material was put on. It would keep sweet and moist for a week, if need be. These crocks, of which there were many, had to have a lid that would not rock, if borne down upon at different points around the edge, or they would not buy them. They were proof against mice and all other pests, and an ant could not run up the outside of one. It was some "good sledding" to pull off a chunk of the hot bread, slap a chunk of butter onto it, which would mostly go into it in a minute, and go to it!

The yeast was made by steeping hops on the stove, not heat-ing very hot, and the liquor mixed with Indian meal, and made into cakes, the shape of codfish cakes, dried, and put up garret in a bag, hung from the rafters, out of Mr. Mouse's way until wanted. After a few years the yeast, which was a distillery byproduct, came around in little cakes, and the old-fashioned kind was abandoned.

WIFE INSTRUCTS HUSBAND VARIOUSLY

The old man gets his orders to get some inside bark from a bass-wood tree: "I want to bottom some chairs that I can stand on when

I whitewash without bellyin' all down, and finally bustin' out. The basswood bark gets as hard as a rock from shrinkin', and that is what I want. The seats in the chairs that Grandpop give us is jes as good as they ever was, even if they have turned black, and if they was painted yeller, they'd look jes like new chairs. They'd be good nuf fer the front room, if the wood on 'em was painted blue." When this inner bark is wet in warm water, and twisted into a small rope, and applied the same as is done with flags in a flag bottom chair, it is the most durable bottom known that has any resilience to it. She certainly knows what she was talking about.

She also said, "If you'll tend to feedin' the pigs, I'll run out to the garden and pull up a mess of them long scarlet short top radishes, and get an apron full of chips at the choppin' block, and then start in gittin' supper. They'll be nice an' brittle, after they lay in cold spring water for a few minutes. Shall I pull up some green onions, too? Tomar I must start in white washin' the celler. It's commencin' to smell musty. Hope you got that line tight, so it ain't air slacked and good for nothin', like you done last spring! And when you come back leave the swill pails out side the pantry, wen the wind's the wrong way, I can smell 'em in the kitchen. Anyhow, the hens will git some good out of pickin' at the sour milk that is stickin' to 'em. They like it as good as you do elder, n' the last time I hung out the close, that old close pole in the yard acted like it was most rotted off. I told you you ought to git locus', but you wouldn't go acrost the brook and cut one.

"You're goin' to get cold corn been tonite, fer supper, and it tain't much good, and I don't expect to hear mutch out of you about it, fur you didn't bring hum Ashton salt as I told you to, an' you know that you can't salt butter, meat, or anything else without it, and heve it good fer anything." She looked around, but he was out of sight, and she started for the garden.

PICKING GEESE

In picking the geese, they were called into a pen by throwing down some corn, and they were caught one at a time as wanted, their legs tied together with a rag (sometimes) and other times neglected

44

to save time, and maybe one would get away, and go over in the back lots, half picked. There was a low chair taken outside at the scene of the operations. The operator would sit down and put the goose on her lap, breast up, left hand holding the feet, and with her right hand quickly tuck the goose's head under her left arm, and then the feathers were pulled out a few at a time with a quick jerk—the quicker they were snatched, the less it hurt. But it hurt aplenty as it was, as the goose scringed every time a pinch of them was pulled. After the position of the left arm with its pressure against the goose's head became tiresome, the tension would relax a little, and the goose would jerk its head out and nip the bare arm. They couldn't bite hard enough with the end of their bill to draw blood, but they could pinch hard enough to make a black and blue spot, and many a time a woman's arm was all spotted from this for three or four days or even a week after the picking was all over. After a goose is picked and thrown down on the yard, it is the most goshawful-looking thing that exists. In appearance it has been dead almost a year, and then has been propped up on its feet. Of course, there is a coating of down left on, or the poor things would maybe chill to death at night, for they are picked quite early in the spring.

When you crawled up on one of those old high bedsteads that you managed to do without a step ladder, and then sank way down almost out of sight in a bed that had forty pounds of live geese feathers in it, and dreamed about almost all the pleasant things imaginable, you were doing it at the expense of a lot of suffering, and it would have served you right if you had dreamed about having your feathers pulled out and it hurt so you had a regular nightmare.

The yaller hangers (Baltimore Orioles) nests that had been hung mostly by pieces of twine given them by the women (sometimes out of their hands) and hair that had gotten out of the horses' tails, were lined to perfection with the feathers that escaped at goose-picking time, and so of course were the homes of the purple martins that used to nest in houses on top of high poles that were built for them. The wrens in their little houses with a hole just big enough for them to get in but keep the sparrows out, and all the other birds helped themselves to feathers for the same purpose.

Looking back to the year of the centennial in '76, and in some cases a few years beyond, my memory is clear about many things that were dying out, and others that have died out since. The raising of flax, and the routine it went through until it was made into linen (Linsey-woolsey) cloth that would scratch your skin, and feel almost as bad as nettles, was one. I only had one trial of it. Cotton cloth, such as streaked shirting, bed ticking, calico, gingham and so on, had reached the country before that time. Many a shirt was made out of bed ticking for winter wear, and a woolen linsey woolsey one over it for very cold weather.

On the next farm they were still raising flax, so I had a chance to see the whole operation, except the weaving. That they had done elsewhere. The ground was prepared the same as for buckwheat, sowed and harrowed in the same. When it was in blossom, it was pretty to look at, with its blue flowers that had a shade of purple mixed in. It was never cut, but always pulled up by the handful, and the dirt beaten off the roots on a rock that was always handy, the roots being cut off after. It was then taken to a large mud puddle, or several of them, where the water got real warm in the sunshine. These puddles were kept full, sometimes by leading a little water off from a brook, or by carrying it in pails. The flax was kept straight as possible, for if it got all snarled up like hay, the after operations worked mean. It was treaded down mostly by barefooted women, so as to let the mud get at all of it, the purpose being to rot the woody part of the spears, the bark or fibrous covering of the woody stalk being the part that linen of all descriptions is made from, even to the white bleached linen sheets. After the woody portion was part rotted so it would break away, it was taken out, washed ("suzzled," as it was called) and dried, keeping it straight as possible. If it was left in the mud too long, so the woody portion could be removed very easily, then the fiber would be weakened some, for it would have begun to rot also. Next it went to the "crakeler," two beams one above the other, and hinged at one end. On the other end the top one had a handle sticking out. Now these beams were so constructed that there were longitudinal slots in the lower one that had longitudinal projections that fitted into it from the upper one, with a rather loose fit. Now, a handful of flax held by one end, the other laid across the lower beam, the upper one was slammed down on it to crakel the woody part. The flax was moved along a little at a time until coming near the end, when the handful would be reversed, and finished, and laid to one side in a pile, still keeping it straight. After this operation, it was taken by the handful and laid across a sharp-edged beam, and struck very near the edge with a hard wood thing that looked like a big thick sword and was called a "swingle"—this to remove still more of the wooden portion. The next operation was to strike it on a "hetchel" and pull, reverse ends, and do the same. This got still more of what wood was left, and also fined up the bark that had little flat places in it. Then it was called "swingletow," and it was a pretty fuzzy mess. They used to call some folks with light fluffy hair "tow heads." Sometimes a part of this swingletow had to have a still further treatment with a comb, and it still had little fine prickers in it.

There is a certain kind of ash whose young trees sometimes have four limbs growing out from a common center, equal distances apart, and after starting out horizontally soon turn upward, the upright limbs being about eight or nine inches apart. A section like this with the body about nine inches long, and the limbs about twice that length, the limbs being about three-quarters of an inch in diameter, and the body one and one-half inches, makes what they call a "distaff." The shank of this distaff is put in a hole in the top of a bench that is the right height, and that is the swingletow holder that the flax is teased from as it is spun. Of course, the flax wheel is a very old appliance, but it is an ingenious machine.

There was a hollow, bell-mouthed spindle that had a hole through the side a ways back from the end. On this spindle, mounted free to turn independently, was a horseshoe-shaped thing called the "flier." It had a lot of hooks on it, and the ends of the horseshoe were pointed towards the outer end of the spindle. There were two grooves in the large driving wheel, one of which lined up with a small grooved pulley that drove the spindle, and the other, the pulley that drove the flier. There were two hard twisted cords of a little over an eighth of an inch in diameter that acted as belts, and were spliced. The one that drove the flier was left so it could slip if the thread getting spun was held a little tight against it, the same being the spinning tension.

In starting, there was a short piece of thread made out of the swingletow, by rolling it on the knee by hand. This was put in the end of the spindle, and out through the side, the end being fastened to one of the hooks on the flier. The wheel was started, and as the twisting began, the swingletow was teased off so as to keep making a thread of uniform size, and after a length was made long enough, the tension was released, and the flier would fly around, and wind it up. When the tension was put on again, the flier stopped and another length was twisted. Thus a continuous thread was made. After there was too much wound around the flier in one place, the thread was shifted to the next hook and another ridge of thread built on, and after the flier had all it could hold, the wheel was stopped, the cord belt thrown off the flier pulley, and the thread taken off with a reel. After there were so many "knots" on the reel, that would make several fliers full. The thread was tied with strings around it at the spaces between the arms of the reel, when it was slipped off the arm of the reel, and was made into a "skein," simply by doubling and twisting it in the hands. When enough of these skeins were on hand, they were weighed, and sent somewhere they had a loom, and they got their linen (linsey-woolsey) cloth in return.

Outside of plowing, and sowing, the women did most of this work, even to helping pull the flax, and believe me, it was a hand-skinning job.

WOOLEN GOODS

The making of woolen goods was something else again. Formerly, they had carded their own wool into "rolls," but the carding mill came around about the time I did, and they used to get it done there. At the carding mill, the wool was thoroughly cleaned, and made into very loosely held-together rolls of almost three-quarters of an inch or less in diameter and five or six feet long, when they were ready for their introduction in the spinning wheel. This wheel was turned by catching hold of a spoke with the hand, and giving it a twirl instead of running it with a foot pedal, as was done with the flax-spinning wheel. This large band wheel, as it was called, was from six to eight feet in diameter and had a thin flat rim about five inches wide. There was no gutter in the face of it, still it was used with a round cord for a belt, the same as the flax wheel, but the pulley that drove the spindle had three deep grooves in it of different diameters, so as to vary the spindle speed. Only one of these grooves was used at a time, of course—the one that happened to suit the operator. The spindle of this wool-spinning machine was solid, about the size of a lead pencil, and projected out from the "spinner head" about nine inches, the head being just high enough to suit the operator, and the elevation of this head adjustable on some spinning wheels.

Now, to begin, a roll was picked up with the left hand, the end of the roll was put around the spindle near (but not on) the end in a way that it ran over itself for a turn or two, the right hand of the operator being on a spoke of the large wheel and just barely moving it until the roll end was bound tight to the spindle. Now here comes the joker. If the left hand was held out to the left when the wheel was turned, the roll of yarn would be twisted, and keep slipping off the end of the spindle every time around. But if the left hand was moved to the right in front of the body, the yarn would be wound to the spindle. When the spinning began, there was a foot or so of the roll between the left hand and the spindle. The big wheel was given a whirl, and the operator ran backwards, maybe twice the length of the spinning wheel, the roll stretching out, and being converted into yarn at the same time. The turning of the wheel, if it was done properly, would not die out until that length of yarn was finished, and the spun portion was wound onto the spindle. This was repeated until that roll was used too near the end, when another was joined to it by merely letting the ends twist together. After the spindle had all the yarn wound on it it could hold, the wheel was stopped, and it was reeled off.

Most of those reels had a click or snap that let you know how many knots, and subdivisions (in some cases), that you had left on the reel. When the desired amount of yarn was on the reel, there were strings tied around the yarn between the arm heads to keep it out of mischief when it was slipped off, made into a skein, later to be cleaned, dyed, weighed, and sent with many others to be woven into homespun (linsey woolsey) cloth that was made into winter bed sheets, and sometimes underclothing for those that had a skin like a rhinoceros.

Of course, some of the yarn was kept for knitting mittens and stockings. These doggoned skeins, after being untied, wanted to twist and tangle everything up. If you were holding a skein in your hands that some old-timer was winding a ball to use at knitting, and you let it slip off your hands, the place for you to get was outdoors, and right quick. There was no use trying to tell her that she gave too hard a twitch on the yarn.

WOMEN—SMOKING

Maybe she might want you to run over to the store, and get her some snuff or something, and that would square everything, and sometimes it was a clay pipe or tobacco, for some of them smoked, and they knew how to take care of their pipes. When one would get black, it was put in the stove over the oven for a week or so, when it would turn white again. It was taken out, and used, and another black one was put in its place.

KNITTING

The old ladies then went to knitting homespun woolen mittens, fifty cents for plain ones, and seventy-five cents for "quail-tracks." I wonder how many there are living today that can knit a quail-track mitten. They would make their fingers fly like lightning, and their tongues just as fast at the same time. A knitting machine was soon in use that would knit a mitten before one of those old women could say, "That is what I said you said you said." Or, at any rate, quick enough to do them out of their knitting pennies. However, the machine has never duplicated that pretty, quail-track pattern.

KNITTING SHEATH ("SHATHE")

A knitting sheath was made of a goose quill and a fancy made-up square and doubled-over piece of woolen cloth, with the edges all scalloped and everything. The large end of the goose quill was opened out, or in other words it was made bell-mouthed.

This 'shathe' was pinned on the waist at the right height, and one end of the knitting needle was inserted in the goose quill, the quill acting as a holder. All knitting was done with four needles. The empty one that was put in the sheath would soon have as many stitches on it as one of the full ones had had, and then of course a needle became bare and was placed in the sheath instead of the one that was full, and so on.

DRESS FASHIONS (MEN'S AND WOMEN'S)

In the dress line, women used to wear a thing they called a bustle. It stuck out to the rear as much as they stuck out in front of it. If a lady was going to make a week's visit, she generally made the bustle up with her clean clothing, and made it up with the soiled ones to go back with.

The hoop skirts had almost died out when I first noticed them. If they had ever come in style again, some of the boys would have been in bad when they were resurrected, for most of the steel springs in them were stolen to make "snap guns" out of. For many years, the style was a big head of hair, the longer the better, on the plan of the seven Sutherland sisters.* If they didn't have long hair, they made out they did by doing it up over a thing called a "waterfall." After that passed out, changes came along fast. They put "rats" in

---

*Editor's note: In the April 1982 issue of *Yankee* magazine Sammarco and Rounds note that the Barnum and Bailey Circus signed them in 1882 and that at the end of their act, "the sisters would turn in unison, letting their voluminous tresses—a collective total of 36½ feet of hair—spill down their backs, over the crest of the stage, and into the orchestra pit. A gasp of amazement and delight would sound through the audience, followed by thunderous applause."

their hair, they had "bangs" in front, "spit curls," braids down the back. A braid twisted around the top of their head like a coiled-up copperhead (chunk head). Then they bobbed it, and now it is a "permanent wave" that the new generation is using. Everything is all curled and jumbled up so that if undesirable tenants should move in, it looks as though it might be hard to get them dispossessed. They will probably shave their heads like a Chinaman the next change, and then those that have to wear a wig will be right in style after they throw it away.

The men's apparel made the women some work—making clothing that they could trade some of their farm produce for, overalls out of blue denim, work pants of Kentucky jean, and sometimes of corduroy—before the canvas overall and work pants made cheaper than they could be at home came out. They used to trade for everything wanted at the general store, and make a settlement every six months. Sometimes the storekeeper would be in the farmer's debt, and sometimes the other way around. Any man that thought himself some punkins had a black dress suit of broad cloth that shined like black glass, and stayed that way if taken care of, until he was buried in it, even though he bought it when he was a young man, and lived to be an old one. The womenfolks had to keep the moths from it with camphor gum that was cheap in those days, not forgetting to keep plenty of it in alcohol. The camphor bottle was brought out to cure most everything. Then there were the dancing pumps, which were rather high-topped boots, made out of calf skin, that had to have a gloss on them from the bottom to the top that you could see your face in if you picked one up to look at it, although they were jet black. A man wasn't supposed to know how to keep them that way, and the women sometimes wore that kind in bad weather, even to a dance. But they were the men's footwear for special occasions—church, weddings, funerals, visiting, dances, going to York, and so on. A few had plug hats made of either silk or beaver fur. The straight ones, or stovepipe-shaped ones, looked good, especially on some, but the kind that belled out at the top looked like—well, never mind. Some had white shirts, and some had a substitute thing they called a dickey, which was nothing but a shirt bosom without the shirt, with a cloth strap to hold it up that buttoned at the back of the neck, with a button that would also button on the collar. When the vest was on, everything looked all right. Finally, they got to wearing cuffs, and later some made of celluloid. It was the habit of some that wore store clothes, a preacher, or maybe a schoolteacher, to wash their cuffs in the morning and set them in the stove with the oven door open part way, so they would dry before sitting down to breakfast. Sometimes, if the oven got hot, they would take fire, starting off with a sort of halfway explosion, and make such a rank black smoke that it would drive everybody out of the house, and there was danger of setting the house afire.

DYEING—CHILDREN'S WORK, ETC.

They used to do their own dyeing of yarn and sometimes cloth. Most of the dyes were "bouten," but some were from native barks. Butternut bark made a nice brown. Brown and blue were the only colors used in stockings and mittens, the blue dye being made from the regular washing indigo and other ingredients. They made each other's dresses, either in silk or calico, buying the goods by the yard. Some were expert needlewomen.

Their kitchen made them plenty of work in many cases. There were large families as a rule, nine children being not uncommon. Of course, as soon as the children were old enough they had to help, both indoors and out, hoeing corn and the like in the fields, and helping with the churning, bringing water, trying out leaf lard, helping with the washing, and maybe learning how to make a minute pudding out of buckwheat flour, and Indian pudding made out of cornmeal instead of rice and baked in the oven, or a hundred and one other things a farm wife would know.

They did a lot of puttering with flowers both outdoors and in the house, and made quite a lot of work for themselves. The hardy perennials like rose bushes, lilacs, snow balls, peonies and so on did not waste much time, but those they had to dig a lot for—merry golds, China aster, youth and old age lady slippers, petunias and per anything you want—did. They seemed to have far better luck with their house plants than those that live in town and run a coal stove. There was one variegated carnation pink plant eighteen inches high and fourteen inches across that had thirty-two flowers on it one Thanksgiving Day, believe it or not. The flowers were so thick on it that it looked like one large bouquet, and the house was all scented up. The neighbors did a lot of gabbing over it, and they were all promised "slips" when the moon got in "perigee" or something, so they would be sure to live. And of course, they had to have a rubber plant, an oleander bush, a Jerusalem cherry tree, and sometimes a little orange tree. The oranges were as pretty looking as they could be, and had a flavor almost as good as a sponge full of water.

The lilacs smelled good, the roses smelled good, and the lily of the valley had a big smell for such a tiny blossom. But if you wanted to get a real fragrance, anchor a boat a rod or two off from the edge of an acre or so of pond lilies when there was just a little breeze blowing from them to you, and throw out your fish line. Chances are your mind would be on the lilies so much, you wouldn't watch your dobber half the time. But you had to have a fish line along to make out you were fishing. Otherwise if other people saw you sitting there just to smell the lilies, they would call you an old woman.

No doubt the Creator of the universe could have made a sweeter-smelling flower than the pond lilies, but there is a doubt that he ever did. It is a scent that the chemists never could catch, or even imitate synthetically.

MAKING SOAP

Soft soap was used for washing clothes entirely until the "rosin" soap came out in bars that were two by three inches square, and a foot long, and sold for eight to ten cents a bar. All pieces of fat, and grease, were saved up, and when the time came in the spring of the year, it was tried out, by being heated in some old large-sized iron pot, or furnace kettle, generally on an outdoors fire, for some of the grease was "ripe," and it smelled to heaven, but after cooking and skimming awhile, it got tamed down to the extent of not smelling at all.

It was then put in the soap barrel a "batch" at a time, and a quantity of lye in proportion as near as could be guessed at, until the barrel was nearly full, and then it was tested by looks and by trial and finished more accurately.

The lye was made in the following manner. The wood ashes were saved, and kept out of the weather all winter. The menfolks put a flat stone up on four other stones so it slanted a little, with a portion that had a partial point to it on the lower side, for the lye to drip off of into a glazed earthen pot. A tight flour or sugar barrel that had a lot of gimlet holes bored through the lower half was set over the low side of the stone. The barrel was somewhat out of plumb, but that did not matter. This barrel was filled with the ashes and a little depression made in the top that would hold about a quart of water. This hole was filled daily with water, and in about a week the lye would begin oozing out onto the stone, and drip off into the earthen receptacle. There was some old oilcloth kept handy so the whole business could be covered up in case of rain. This lye was powerful stuff. It would eat a hole through your skin if it got a chance, and if it was boiled until dry it made potash, which the people had very little use for, except to eat a wart off a horse, and stop its eating with vinegar, or maybe daub it around rat holes so they would get it on their feet and leave. This soap barrel had to have a sassafras stick to stir the soap with, so as to scent the soap. This soap is the slipperiest stuff imaginable. There was some sale for it at one time, to put on the runway when a boat was to be launched. If some gent came "perlaverin'" around trying to put something over, he would probably be told, "You can't soft soap me."

LIGHTING FACILITIES

More than half the country people had not got to the kerosene stage yet in the early seventies. All they had for indoor light was dipped candles, and in case they ran out, they used a thing called a "slut," which was nothing more than a rag with one end of it drawn in a large button and put in a saucer of tallow. It didn't make much light, and most of what it did make went up to the ceiling. A bright bake tin propped up at the right angle would reflect enough light to see fairly well by. And for outdoors, all the light they had was a tin lantern, merely a cylinder punched full of holes, and a candle in it. It is surprising how much light one of them will throw through the little holes, and the strongest wind will not blow the candle out. The holes were sometimes punched in geometrical designs, or maybe a star or crescent, and a dog's head, or something. A fellow that had one like that was supposed to be putting on airs, for it cost five or ten cents more.

There was an effort made to supplant candles that "died abornin'." It was a cone-shaped tin affair, with the apex of the cone cut off so as to screw in a plug cap that had two round tubes sticking up about an inch, and an inch apart at the bottom. They flared out from each other at a small angle. There was a round stick in each of these, and the lamp burned "camphene." It made a fine light, but one of them after being used a short time exploded, and it was nip and tuck to keep the house from burning down. The news traveled by grapevine telegraph, and they were never used again.

A few months after, a salesman came through to introduce kerosene, and he was nearly kicked out of some of the houses. They told him they "didn't want anything around the house that had an 'ene' to it." They had had one experience in the neighborhood and that was enough. He showed them a lighted match plunged into kerosene would go out, and then they were sure he was a faker. "If it won't burn when you touch a match to it, do you think anybody is going to believe it will crawl all the way up the wick and burn on top?" He filled a lamp and lit it, and they acted that they would rather he would have done it outdoors. He sold one lamp, or left it on trial, and the party that bought it put it out in the smoke house to burn all night "to see if it will bust or not afore mornin'."

In dipping candles there was a deep pot of melted tallow that was only about hot enough to stay melted. The candlestick was doubled and twisted lightly, the loop end having a wire or stick passed through it. Several of these were put on one stick about three inches apart and out on the "stoop," or outside anyhow. There were two sawhorses, with poles put on them, and fastened the right distance apart for the sticks or wires to rest on with the candles hanging down between. The weather had to be quite cold to have things work out right. The first part was the worst, that of getting a start. Some hung small weights on the end of the wicks to get a start, but they became a nuisance afterwards. The best way was to get a coating of tallow on the wicks any old way, by punching them under with a stick or something. Then they were pulled up quickly, and with the thumb and finger of the other hand the wicks pulled down straight. Some did this barehanded, and some got their thumb and finger burned. It was better to wear a buckskin glove or something. After they were straightened, you walked out and put the stick across the poles, carrying a bake tin under the embryo candles to catch the drip. You may have had to straighten some a second time, before they get enough tallow on them to keep them straight. If you had a lot of these sticks, you could take them in rotation, and keep going. They were to be gotten as cold as possible outside, and shoved in the tallow and out, as quickly as possible, or there would be as much melted off as got on. The big end of the candle was the lower end, the loop end was the one lighted, the reverse of a molded candle. They were sort of lumpy on the outside, but they gave a better light than a molded candle. They stopped dipping when the top end was about three-quarters of an inch in diameter, and the bottom would be about an inch and an eighth. Some made them a foot, and some made them fourteen inches long.

One day in came a thing that would "Yep, make six candles all to once!" And later on they got one that made a dozen, and it was the talk of the neighborhood.

They had so much trouble with lamp chimneys, for years, that candles were used as much as lamps, and they serve as "pinch hitters" yet. So far as the light itself is concerned for desk work, the old student lamp with its Argand burner* is as good as any, electric

---

*Editor's note: The Argand burner was developed in France in the late eighteenth century. A round hollow wick was surrounded by a cylindrical tube, and air flowed through and around the wick and then up through the cylindrical chimney to increase the supply of air to the flame.

not excepted. But it is nasty to take care of, and throws too much heat for summer use.

MATCHES AND FIRE

The old flint and steel and some tinder in a book were up garret, but were never used to make fire except to show how it could be done to some that wanted to see it. Tinder was made by burning some old pieces of linen that were getting beyond their usefulness for other purposes. It was very delicate after being burned. It left a black semi-ash, the same shape the cloth was before burning. It stuck together with just enough tenacity to allow handling carefully, and that is why it was kept between the leaves of a book. It had the quality of catching fire from a spark, and the fire would go crawling around slowly, but no flame. It was carefully brought together in a loose lump after being sparked, and this lump was put on a layer of swingletow, or maybe the frazzly bark of a red cedar tree that was folded over it, to make a sort of ball. It would burst into a flame sometimes, by merely blowing on it, but the safest way was to use a little wire basket hung on a wire about two feet long, and put the ball in it, and swing the thing in the air. The rush of air through the ball would make it flame, and of course, it was then applied to some inflammable wood shavings or straw, as the beginning of a regular fire.

The first matches that could be depended upon if kept dry were round sticks with dark blue heads. They were in a box that was a bar rail gray, that had a lid that shoved down over the end of the box, about one-third its length. The box was shaped like a cylinder that had been smashed down about one-third its diameter. The box sold for four cents, generally, and it had a three-cent government tax stamp on it, so the tax was three times what the matches and box cost. If you enjoyed a smell that would make the leaves fall off the trees for rods around, you got your money's worth when you lit one, and it was such a durable smell. It would get away down somewhere about the middle of you, and stick around for an hour or two. But those matches had one virtue: if saliva was put on warts, and then rubbed with the head of one of them, at night, when going to bed, in a few days the warts would be gone. This was pooh-poohed by some, but there were so many warts removed, and no failures, that it finally became an established fact.

Then came out yellow-headed square-sticked things that didn't amount to much as far as lighting was concerned, but they did not have such an awful smell. They were used in the parlor. But the blue heads were used in the kitchen, where you wanted a fire when you wanted it, and didn't want to rub, rub, rub three or four that wouldn't light at all, and then get one that would fizz a little and go out before you could do anything about it. Then came the parlor matches that made a noise like a snapping gun cap when one went off, and maybe the head all aflame would fly across the room and set fire to something. They had some sharp sandpaper on the box to strike them on. The Swedish safety match and others as well as the paper things that keep on burning when you throw them down are present-day stuff.

HOUSE CAT

The house cat has been condemned by those who are misinformed as being a great game killer. A cat catches young rabbits, chipmunks, and both wood and meadow mice, and rarely a bird of any kind in the country proper, though the town cat will catch chickens and sparrows, and even pigeons. When there were lots of farmers, and lots of cats, there was lots of game. To this day there is more game near some of the farmhouses than anywhere else, and it is not an uncommon sight to see the cat sitting on the garden wall, waiting for a chipmunk to come along, and a flock of quail within a few feet of her, picking bugs in the garden, and when she walks through a flock of young chickens, she pays no attention to them.

It is a poor way to get permission to hunt on a farmer's place, to advocate killing any cats that are in the woods. When the farmer gets wise to what they think about cats killing game, he saves arguments and explanations by posting his farm against hunting. It is much simpler for some writer to rehash some story that has been started, than it is to live in the country fifty or sixty years, to know what he is writing about.

A cat is great company for the housewife when she is alone, and she and the rest of the family become attached to the cat to such an extent that they wouldn't grieve any more if the best cow on the yard was killed than they would if the cat was killed. Some cats are funny. There was one that every time a stranger came to the house, and she was inside, she would hide without anybody seeing her under something that was as far from the door as possible. After everything had settled down, and the conversation had been running along for maybe fifteen or twenty minutes, someone might open the door, and BANG, out she came, with an awful squall, every hair sticking straight out from her tail, and she flew across the floor and out. Everybody would give a jump, the same as they would if the house had busted wide open. Nobody could say anything for a second or two, and then maybe someone would say, "Damn that cat!" And then everybody would have a good laugh, and the cat was probably around the corner of the house having a cat laugh. There was no use trying to get used to her. She pulled that stunt off so suddenly that she would get you every time.

Another one used to clear the womenfolks out of the kitchen screeching, by bringing in a snake that was wriggling all around her. After someone got hold of a beanpole, or something, and chased her out of the kitchen, she would go out on the lawn and let the snake go again, and then strut off, as though she was well pleased with herself. And then they will tell you that a cat has no sense of humor. Some have quite a bit of intelligence. One old cat used to drop her kittens around the neighborhood, and then come around and peek from a distance to see how each kitten was being treated, and without letting the kitten see her. If the kitten was fed, and being treated all right, after a week or so, she would not be sneaking around any more. Any kitten that wasn't being treated right was taken somewhere else.

VI

Life of the
Rocky Farm Men

PLANTING

If it was corn, the seed corn that was of the choicest ears had been hung up the fall before by the house from the wires that crossed from rafter to rafter near the peak in the garret. Corn was not suggested to be shelled until just before the planting, to get the best results. Sometimes corn was sent off and exchanged with someone at a distance, or maybe new seed was bought, sometimes from Canada. But there was never any field corn raised except the flint variety, generally the long-eared, eight-rowed kind, meaning that there were eight rows of grain on the cob. The Canadian flint corn, however, had more rows and the ears were shorter.

The corn was shelled out and put in water to soak all night the day before. A bag of plaster (ground gypsum), a bag of the wet corn, a six-quart dropping pail, two old tomato cans, one for citron seeds and one for pumpkin seeds, a keg of water, two eight-quart ash pans, the hoes, etc. were taken to the field, which had been furrowed with a corn plow, the furrows being four feet apart, the plow being drawn by one horse. These furrows were to be cross-furrowed, or marked also four feet apart, and at right angles to the plowed furrows. A corn plow is a small, one-handled and one-handed plow, with the crook of the handle turned forward instead of to the rear, as the two handles of the regular, full-sized 2½ D. plow is.

The reins were adjusted so they were not too tight nor too loose, and slipped over the plow handle, and let to drop below the crook, where they rested on a stop. The plowman grasped the plow handle above the reins at the crook with his left hand (if he was right-handed) and with his right hand he reached the reins, and slipped them around right or left to guide the horse. If he tried to carry the reins in his right hand, his arm would soon get tired out.

The plaster was a fertilizer used around corn a good bit, and particularly to increase the growth of grass on meadows. Its worst feature was that it got all over everything when sown broadcast, unless a no-wind time was picked out.

Now we will say there are four of us, which makes a handy crew for the business at hand. We will start operations. The fellow that does the cross-furrowing starts off first to get ahead of the rest, and stay ahead for the day. He has a rope tied to about four feet of quite heavy chain, which he drags after him to "make his mark in the world." By the time he has at least two furrows finished, most of the wet corn has been rolled in dry plaster and put in the dropping pail, the pumpkin and citron seed in the cans, all slung by a small rope over the shoulder, and we are off. There are four grains dropped at each corner or crossing, dropping two rows at a time, and at every fourth pair of hills a pumpkin seed is put in with the corn, on one row, and a citron seed on the other. If a grain of corn strikes a stone and bounces away, it must be picked up for fear the crows will find it and get started to pull the corn when it comes up. These black rascals get so wise sometimes that they will set up on a scarecrow that is enough to scare a man, and caw at you, until you get within a hundred yards of them.

The hoe men, or coverers, are following right along after the dropper, each one taking a row. After they put a hoeful of dirt on each hill, they pat it with the back of the hoe. Sometimes where the corn is dropped in a small space between the stones, the coverers have to hunt around a step or two to get a hoeful of dirt to bring and put on it, and if the furrowing chain happens to cross the plowed furrow right where the hill ought to be, and there is a stone occupying the space, the dropper is supposed to try and move it out of the way. If he can't, that hill will be vacant, or properly speaking, there will be no hill there at all.

Now, after the dropper has been at it for half a day, the ends of his fingers will begin to hurt, for the lime element in the plaster that the corn is coated with will have eaten through the skin. There is no use trying to tie your fingers up with rags and get along. You wouldn't make more headway than a cat in mittens catching mice. Your only remedy is to change work with one of the hoe men, and he will have to do the same later on.

The planting of potatoes was similar, except pieces of potatoes with a certain number of chits or eyes on each piece were dropped plain, or with a little patent fertilizer, and both crops had to be furrowed first one way, and the next, at right angles, until furrowed three times, with the corn plow, and of course hoed each time. There were two furrows made between the rows, the moldboard throwing towards the hills, which were always to the right. The last time through was called "hilling." In the case of corn, it was sometimes as high as the horse's back, and as the hills were supposed to be made large, there was a scrabble for dirt. Sometimes the plow would slither a stone to one side that would slice off a hill, or maybe roll on it, and mast it as flat as a griddlecake. When the men with the hoes came along, they were expected to handle this proposition the best they could. Sometimes the spears would have a kink in them, and be too weak to stand up without dirt being banked around them, but it didn't pay to waste too much time over these cripples on a two-stone-to-one dirt farm.

They believed in planting everything that grew out of the ground on the new of the moon, and everything that grew in the ground on the old of the moon. Sometimes pole beans that were planted on the old of the moon would refuse to run up the poles. They would grow up a foot or so, and be reaching off in the air, as if they wanted to go away and grow somewhere else. Corn should not be planted until white oak leaves are as big as a crow's foot. If planted earlier, it will come up, and get stunted, and some that is planted maybe two weeks later will grow right past it, and produce a better crop. If the crows got very troublesome pulling young corn, they stretched a string all around the cornfield on sticks, and it was quite some work. But if a crow happened to fly over it before he saw it, he would immediately reverse, and go right back the way he came, apparently very much frightened. They appeared to think it was a trap.

The "taters" were planted much earlier than corn, on the old of the moon, and on the patches that showed some semblance of being land. But even then there were many potatoes grown out of shape, trying to make a stone "hitch over" to get room. They had to have the same cultivation as the corn, of course.

SOWING GRAIN

The sowing of grain was by broadcasting it by hand, and it was a knack that could only be learned by a lot of practice, and many never did learn to do it properly. Assuming a man was right-handed, the bag was at the left side, with a small rope from each end of the bag passing over the right shoulder. The attachment at the lower end was made by choking off about a handful of grain in the corner, and tying tight between it and the bag proper. This was the "knob," and it prevented the rope from slipping off. The upper open end could be fastened by folding over a little stone, and tying below it. These two attachments being in line with each other, the bag could be carried at any angle across the body, so as to make it handy to reach into with the right hand. By partially opening the fingers a certain way as the arm was swung around, the first of the grain would strike the ground about six feet to the right, and six feet at the front of the inside edge of the semicircle or near semicircle the grain covered. From the inner edge to the outer edge was about four feet. After two gauged steps forward, that were acquired by practice, the next handful was cast, and so on across the field. When the grain came up, it appeared to be perfectly uniform, with the edge of grain that had been sown before as his guide. But in sowing buckwheat, there were "monuments" set up, and moved over twelve feet every time the field was crossed, and sometimes where there was a knoll in the field, there had to be one put on top of it. There were "balks" in some fields that had to be worked around, and they were a nuisance. There were islands in the field that were nothing but a lot of rock and bramble that could not be tilled, and were used to throw stones on that were taken off the surrounding field.

When the grain was all sown, the team was hooked to a bush harrow, which was drawn all over the field, and covered most of the grain with dirt, and dragged the grain off that had landed on the stones. A bush harrow was nothing but a tree about as big as a stovepipe, that had plenty of limbs on it. Sometimes corn was sown this way for fodder, and if there was an enlarged patch of sweet corn raised the year before, a little for the table and the balance sown, the cattle liked it much better. The sweet corn patch had to be remote from the flint corn, or they would mix.

SWAMPS AND MARSHES— CRANBERRIES, BLUEBERRIES, GARDEN TRUCK

On most of the farms there was a swamp or two, even though the farm was near the top of a mountain. They were pockets that were formerly little lakes, that had gradually filled up with decayed vegetation, commonly called muck, and on this muck, bogs (warts on the earth) had grown. They were generally about thirty inches high, eighteen inches in diameter and about two feet apart on the average. In a dry time, they could be cut with a float hoe, or bog hoe. It is really an overgrown adz, with the blade about fourteen inches long. By cutting all around the bog so the cut reached the center at the bottom, it could then be toppled over. They were drawn off the swamp, to some out-of-the-way place on the upland, and burned later, after they dried out. Then there was a main ditch cut all the way across the swamp from the highest to the lowest point, if there wasn't a brook running through it already. Then there were a lot of cross ditches cut out to the main ditch, or brook, as the case may be. These cross ditches were dug about three feet deep, and stones about the size of a man's head thrown to the bottom to a depth of about eighteen inches. The ditch was then filled with enough of the muck to make it flush with the surroundings, and the surplus was taken away. This was known as "blind ditching," as the plow ran right over the ditch, and for five or six years, if wood ashes were sown on and plowed under to neutralize the sourness of the soil, enormous crops could be raised. Unfortunately, these ditches stopped up after a few years. It is too bad that porous tile pipe was unknown then, or they might have stayed dry enough to till for an extended period. After the bogs had been off the swamp for long enough to till it, it got dry sometimes, for when they were on it, they acted like a sponge to hold water in a dry time.

When there was a brook that could be dammed up nights, and the water let out days, if need be, that was fine business, and you were all set to raise bumper crops of potatoes, onions, and strawberries, and it was by this rotation that a certain man made enough money in five years to let himself and his wife down easy in their old age. It was a seven-acre swamp, and all he had to help him was two daughters and one small Canadian horse. There are trees some fifty feet high here and there, and the rest a thick jungle of native stuff on that swamp today. It is peculiar that these swamps never go to bogs after they have once been tilled. Those swamps if put in shape will produce as good now as they ever did.

But "the cream is off the milk." The price of garden truck and strawberries is now so low, and worse than all, no children to pick them, that there is nothing to it. Formerly our native berries got to our local markets first. Now the people are all fed up on strawberries from Florida, or some other place, by the time our vines start to bud. The gigantic and slick system of producing, refrigerating, expressing, and handling garden truck today, from the time the fast trains leave from right in the garden until it reaches your back door, has got all the small-fry garden truck producers backed off the map. They have the finest, richest stoneless and irrigated soil when needed, along with cheap labor, and all kinds of machinery. Rather than try to make a living by raising garden truck to sell in towns and cities, the rocky farmer might better crawl around the barn and die.

What little the farmer and peddler handle helps to curb the stores some. It would hardly do to let the stores reign supreme. The people used to watch the weight and quality of the produce they bought, and if it wasn't up to standard, they would shove it back the same as they would a pair of stockings in a store if one had a hole in it. Nowadays, they take whatever they get, and say nothing. Barnum said, "There is a fool born every minute." He was wrong, there are two!

There is another form of swamp that is of an entirely different formation, called a "cranberry marsh." One of these in particular I will try to describe. Originally, they were lakes, and some of them are part lake yet, like this one. There is a long-rooted moss that starts to grow around the hard ground shore, and gradually spreads out over the water, and after a while is capable of holding anyone up that walks on it, the roots being from five to seven feet long, including the dead portion at the bottom. Near shore, the roots strike bottom, but after the water gets more than seven feet deep, they form a floating interlaced mat. Your feet will sink in it to your ankles, but don't worry, for it is a job to even force a pole down through it. If you jump up and down, anyone on the marsh can feel the movement fifty yards away.

It is on these marshes that cranberries and pitcher plants grow. This swamp now shows three stages of vegetation evolution, which I will call rings, and a lake. The first ring, of about a two-hundred-yard width from the hard ground out, is covered with quite big timber. Some trees are near a hundred feet tall, and when the wind blows, the roots rise and fall to comply with the strain, and anyone between the trees will have the sensation of being on a boat that is being tossed about by the waves. The next ring inside this one is some twenty-five yards wide from inside to outside edge and covered mostly with blueberry or swamp huckleberry bushes, some so large that a man can climb up in them. This ring also has an inside fringe of about fifty feet of huckleberry bushes of a different kind, that are about waist high and bear berries that shine and look like jet black glass beads, and they are so sweet no sugar need be used with them. Next, there is a ring of regular cranberry marsh that is about fifty yards from outside edge to inside edge, like that which first formed at the shore of the lake in ages gone by. There is a little lake in the center, of sixty yards in diameter. This lake has decreased in diameter something like a foot a year during the last fifty years, and all the rings have closed in proportion. Eventually, if nothing changes the present routine, the marsh will cover the lake, later the huckleberry bushes will cover the marsh, and still later, the big timber will take the place of the huckleberry bushes, and there will be a forest over a sunken lake. If a pole is shoved down through the marsh and worked up and down so as to make a practically clean hole, the water will rise up in it to near the top, the same as it does when you make a hole through the ice on a frozen-over body of water. You can let a lead sinker on a line through this hole fifty feet before it will reach the mud bottom, and nobody knows how deep the mud is. The moss rots and the mud is reddish yellow in color. The sunfish in this lake are the most gorgeous colored of any fish I know of, and the colors are so sharply defined, in contrast to sunfish that have pale colors, and [sort] of mix in with the adjacent ones when they come together in the regular lakes about the country. However, neither they nor the pickerel from the marsh lake are fit to eat. They have a nasty rotten vegetable taste, and the pond shiners caught in this lake through the ice with a drop net and taken to other lakes to be used as bait will catch no fish, for they will not be touched.

But, oh boy—the blueberries! They grow in great profusion. A city fellow was told to go up a small tree and see what he could see. He came down all excited and said he could see acres that were all blue. He wanted to know if anybody would kick if a large quantity of these berries were picked, and when he was told no, he said he was going to get a lot of kids to pick them, and ship them to the city, and make some money. But when all the ins and outs were explained to him, he became normal again. It appears to be destined to have many tons of these berries go to nothing, so far as man is concerned—although it looks to be possible for a few young fellows to take a small portable canning outfit to the hard ground near one of these marshes, and come away with a small lot of canned blueberries if they are not greenhorns, know how to use an axe, and how to know good spring water. There wouldn't be any money in it, but there would be a lot of fun, and a blueberry pie or a pudding in the wintertime is good enough sledding for anybody. The secret of having berries taste natural is to get them right off the bushes and into the cans. They won't be so good in two hours after they are picked.

Might as well give you the rest of it. Get a round bake tin that has a didimus that loosens anything from the bottom when you run it around. Throw enough blueberries in the tin to cover the bottom half an inch or more, level off, and do the same with the same bulk of sugar. Make the same kind of batter that you use for a layer cake, and put it on the berries and sugar, and bake. Run the didimus to loosen everything from the bottom. Turn over on a platter with the berry, or bottom side up, and go to it! Better not give any of it to the company that you don't care to see very often, for if they find out you have more berries around, they will be right back.

Along in the seventies, some cranberries from this marsh created some excitement in the neighborhood. One old woman said to another, "They are eating cranberries!" "Go on!" "Yes, they are! I sold some and they paid me for them." "For land sakes! What in tarnation will they be eating next? I bit into one once, and it was sour enough to make a pig squeal, and puckered my mouth all up!"

There was quite a few dollars' worth taken from that swamp, by some poor widows, but they were hard earned, for they had to lug them eight miles on foot, as the old road had very few wagons traveling on it. These berries were not used by country people for twenty years after that, and very seldom to this day by the old-timers. For some reason late years they do not grow there any more to speak of, and nobody cares. Of course they were used by city and some town folks. They started in cultivating them in sections of the U.S. that were suitable, and they were shipped all over the country in barrels.

Editor's note: The following related material is taken from one of Barger's letters to his daughter Flossie.

Your remark about the cranberry swamp is a point well taken, if I did not mention the fact that the cranberries grew on the moss, and also the pitcher plant. Of course most everybody knows there is no bush cranberries in this country, or at least I never heard of any. You can inject that somehow.

There is another thing about the swamp if you want to extend the book. A forest of trees over a sunken lake is not the last stage of those swamps as I see it. It is my belief that in ages to come the growth and decay will finally fill up that lake, and the timber will all die off, and a log swamp will remain. That appears to be the last stage, for you can go on any log swamp, and either dig down, or drive a spear down, and you will connect with "Bog Oak," or some other kind of timber. Just over the hill in Jersey from where you were born, they have a big machine that they spear large trees away down in the muck, and very slowly bring them to the surface, and they are used to make lead pencils. They were of cedar, some as big as a barrel, and near a hundred feet long, but they had no scent. In Put. Co. all we find is black as ink and is oak of some kind judging by the grain, and they are so hard that a nail is hard to drive in them, cheap smoking pipes are made of them.

POISON SUMAC AND POISON IVY

These swamps have poison sumac in them that never bothers the country people any, but does a few from the cities and towns. Those who are susceptible to it, or who are afraid that they are, should wash in strong soapsuds on coming out of the swamp. If hot water can be had, so much the better. If any itching and little pimples show up, rub on alcohol, or gasoline. Common kerosene will work on most people.* Every one of the little pimples should be picked open with a needle while they are wet with the dope and plenty rubbed in after. If the contents of the blister get on the bare skin, the pimples will spread. The poison is supposed to be an oil, and must be diluted, and washed away. This poison, and poison ivy, is mostly a joke to the majority of people. They are affected with it a little a time or two, and become immune. Many never are affected at all. Both these poisons are practically the same, and also the remedy. The sumac is somewhat more virulent, but less apt to attack. Some pick berries where it grows, and push it aside without its affecting them, and the same ones will be attacked by the ivy.

It is rare, but just the same some people seem to be a regular marker for poison ivy and are affected with it even in the wintertime. Burning the vines of ivy and letting the smoke strike you, or inhaling it, is bad medicine, and some have almost lost their lives this way.

A case occurred within the last five years that should be mentioned. A man riding along the road saw some vines on a stone wall that he thought would be good for his goat to eat. He took some along and the next day he was all broken out on his face and hands with poison ivy blisters. He sought the advice of an old woman. She told him what it was, and that if he would make a tea of the vines, and drink it, he would never have it again. He did it, and she was right—he died.

There was a poor family years ago that came from the city to try to make a living in the country, and not knowing any better, cut some poison sumac along with the rest of their firewood. The stove smoked, they inhaled the smoke, and more than half the family died. The rest came very near it, and maybe never got entirely over the effects of it. Those that lived went back to the city.

Let me warn you that if you are very susceptible to poison ivy, and if the conditions are right—if you are perspiring a little, and there is a mild air current moving from the vines to you, at a time

---

*Editor's note: Readers are discouraged from following this advice.

when it is throwing off a lot of its poison, which it does most in July—you can get poisoned by it if you get within ten feet of it. This has been proven absolutely. There is nothing mysterious about it. Did you ever pass by a rose bush, maybe ten or twenty feet from it, and get the fragrance from the roses? And did you know that it is minute particles of oil that are floating in the air that give you the sensation? Now, the poison vine is sending off minute somethings, and because they have no odor, you do not get wise to them, for the time being at least. It may be found out that they are spores or germs that propagate and spread like those of a contagious disease, when they reach suitable soil. If it is a poison, it is the only kind of poison that can multiply itself so many million times, and spread from a little pimple to all over the place. Strychnine couldn't do that. If attacked on only a small area, get busy and keep it from spreading. You know the best way to keep a dog from running mad in August is to shoot him in July.

FARMER'S BREAKFAST

These farmers sure have to do an awful lot of hard work, and if they did not know enough to eat a substantial breakfast, they never could stand it. The farmer was brought up with the understanding that he must never eat anything sweet before eating meat, and other heavy food, as it would take his appetite away. Breakfast should be the heaviest meal of all. The stomach has had the longest rest, and will perform its function without giving one an overloaded feeling like a big meal will if eaten any other time of day. Mark Twain said, "Never do anything before breakfast, but if there is anything that you must do before breakfast, then eat your breakfast first." Here is a piece of sound sense, garnished with nonsense.

If a solid man has solid work to do, he must have a solid breakfast, and get fixed for the day, if he expects to stay solid. Of course if a man does nothing, thinks nothing, and amounts to nothing, he can live on nothing for breakfast—for a while.

Some conniving boarding house missus in the past invented a scheme to try on the hall room boys. She gave them some kind of mattress filling, the first thing in the morning, with some sugar on it, and got away with inveigling them into thinking they had had a breakfast. They naturally could not eat much else after the sugar, and the cereal puffed them up enough to fool them. Some doctors say this is fine business. Maybe it is for them. You don't have to believe everything the doctors tell you. Don't they tell you that they are trying to eradicate all the diseases of mankind? Catch them doing it, if they could. If they did that, they wouldn't be able to make enough stuff with puffed, fluffed stuff enough to keep the insides of their intestines from growing together.

Don't [allow] all this habit to get the best of you. If you keep on fooling your stomach, your stomach will fool you some day. Stop gorging yourself evenings, and cut out that dried-up lunch in the middle of the day, or the grab-and-swallow "what is it" at some stand. You will soon learn to eat a real meal in the morning, and another in the evening, doing your day's work in between. There is no better system for health and convenience.

The fellow that gave his horse old newspapers and put green goggles on him, so he would think them hay, nor the one that crossed his bees with lightning bugs so they could see to work night and day, was no meaner than the inventor of this fake breakfast. Maybe the woman is too lazy to get up and cook a man his breakfast nowadays, in the towns and cities. But they should eat the same way themselves. There is no lunch to put up, and only two washings of dishes, instead of three each day. Of course, when the city folks come out in the country to board, they get this same kind of rip sawdust, chomped oak leaves, and whatever they want, that the cereal companies put up, though the country people don't bother with them.

COMPARISON OF WESTERN AND EASTERN FARMING

The western farmer has the laugh on his eastern brother rock fighter. He sits up on his power machine, having a regular joy ride comparatively, and one of them that went out west from one of these rocky farms wrote back that he didn't like to farm it where a fellow has to load his corn in a shot gun, and shoot it in between the stones to plant it.

It is true that the western farmer has troubles of his own, and did, even before the tractor was thought of. Some years the corn would be in piles the size of houses, and it could not be sold for enough to pay for hauling it away, not did it pay to fatten stock with it. The only use that was made of it was to use it for fuel, and a little for home consumption, fattening stock with it included. Right now, it would not do to raise all the grain and fatten all the stock that could be, with all the modern appliances that are at hand, or the markets would be glutted. They are near enough to it now, so far as the farmer is concerned.

VII

SPORTS AND ANIMALS

HUNTING

Up to about 1912, these rocky farms were probably as good a place as any in the United States to hunt the "partridge," now called the "lordly grouse," although we hunters used to call him the devil now and then. If there is anything that lives on this earth with a brain anywhere near as small as theirs that can outwit a man (and sometimes a bunch of men) any slicker than a partridge can, I have yet to see, read or hear about it. In some sections, like in the state of Maine, they are either trustful or dumb. But there is only an exceptional one dumb around these old rocky farms. It makes the sportiest shooting there is, because it is the hardest. In the olden times they used to lie for a dog, but they got so wise that the most of them would rise a hundred yards away if they saw a dog. So they had to be walked up. Sometimes they will fly behind you, and when you wheel around they will be flying right at your face. You duck down a little, and the partridge slants up a little, just enough to clear the top of your head. You try to shake off the shock, straighten up and turn around quick, you seem to get tied in a knot, and by the time you get untied, the bird is out of sight. It will be the first time you found out how clumsy your feet are—you and your gun got around first, somehow. After a fellow has had several hunting seasons' experience, shot off several young saplings, and a few holes in the sides of trees, if it is in him to control his nerves, and become a good partridge shot, he will probably kill half he shoots at, taking every chance where he can see the bird for ten feet or more, before it goes behind something that cannot be shot through, and also quick snap shots at those that dive in the leaves of trees. Waiting for open shots spoils all the fun. You may not get one out of a dozen rises. Most people do not like to fire a lot of shots without getting anything, or maybe one bird or so, but it has got to be done! If a fellow ever learns to shoot partridges, after he is a good average shot he may strike a streak of hard luck, and fire maybe half a dozen times without getting anything, and get plagued about it when he comes out of the woods by some of the neighbors. They may ask him when the war started.

There are some wounded ones lost, and it cannot be helped. Sometimes one will fly an eighth of a mile and drop dead, and at other times in picking birds, it is found that gangrene has set in from a previous wound that they would have soon died of. Changing guns is bad! Get one that you can slam to your shoulder very quick, pulling the trigger the instant it strikes, that will throw the shot right where you are looking. This is snap shooting. If you have a little more time, use it, by giving your gun an instantaneous look to see where it is. If the aim needs correcting, twitch it over, and let her go. This is a delayed snap. If you have plenty of time, bring your gun on the job slower, and steadier, which only takes a fraction of a second.

A good axeman has to have his axe hung just so, and he doesn't like to use anyone else's axe, for it throws him off his aim when he comes back to his own. A man that uses a scythe that is a good mower must have it hung just so, and even a machinist's hammer, if it does not hang just so, he cannot do good work with it. A man with a broad axe that is hung to suit him can split the chalk line all day, and get out sticks of timber that look as though they were planed. These axes weigh about twelve pounds. It is the hang of the tool, and the familiarity with it that is the secret of taking aim, be it with an axe or a gun.

After your gun becomes a part of yourself, and you have gotten your nerves hardened, so they won't get your goat with that thunder of theirs when they explode in the air, you will be able to get a partridge now and then. It won't do any good to feel like kicking yourself after the bird has disappeared. They do these things as a delightful stunt. They must have some substitute for laughing. It is the grandest sport in the land, but it has gone beyond the reach of the rather poor man. There is only one way now, and that is to find someone that has partridge on his place, and then say to him, "I won't set fire to your woods. I won't shoot any of your stock, your fowls, your cat, nor tear down any fence, and I will give you five dollars for a day's hunt." He may have a friend or two that he is saving his birds for. He may be a partridge hunter and saving them for himself. Or he may be one of those that think that partridges are sacred, and turn you down.

Never go with more than one besides yourself, and if you know enough about the woods to keep from getting lost, better go alone, or maybe some country lad without a gun consent to go with you, and if he is the right sort, you will find more birds with him than you would alone. But if you are one of those fellows than cannot concentrate on your job as well when anybody is present, go alone, or take him once to get familiar with the lay of the land, and go it on your own in after trips. The game on a man's farm is as much an asset as the apples on his trees. If he threw open his orchard, and his forest, how long would he have any apples, or any game? Or, for that matter, anything else. They would do all kinds of damage. Put yourself in the farmer's place, and think from his standpoint.

Woodcock is probably the choicest bit of flesh that nature ever produced, but they are small, and except an odd one, are rather easy to shoot. They are so scarce on the general average except up New Brunswick way, that there is not enough sport attached to them. Our local bred birds start to migrate at the same time they do way up in New Brunswick, and have gone south before the law is up to shoot them. We only get the few stragglers that keep coming, until after freezing weather sometimes, and a one-day stopover is generally their limit. You may run across a few, and go back next day looking for more—you won't find a bird. Quails are hardly worth mentioning, nobody bothers to hunt them much anymore. I doubt that there is one quail shot for every five square miles of this eastern territory, each season. They are scarce and small. They just don't fit or they would increase. Ducks and geese were scarce, and are nearly gone now. Now and then there was a little shooting at the small lakes, but laying hid waiting to get a shot, when the lake would be frozen over if the wind would give it a chance, is not hunting—that is freezing! Similar to fox hunting, except that in fox hunting you freeze standing up, waiting for the hounds to bring the fox around. Both are silly ways to commit suicide, by way of pneumonia. Cooning, that is different, you have something to keep your blood in circulation, and something that you take great pleasure in, once you catch the fever, or perhaps it ran in the family, and you were lucky enough to be born with it.

When "Old Towser," the leader of the coon hound orchestra, starts his musicians playing a piece, and the strains float across country, the audience comes to quick attention and listens to the harmony. At the end of the piece, they all tune up their instruments until the ring-tailed gentleman that did the dancing for the show has been attended to. When they go looking for another inspiration to start the band playing again, while the curtain is down, the audience has a chance to pick up their torn breeches, pick some cat briers out of their hide, and pour the water out of their boots before the next act. These wild woods theatricals beat them all! "Weber and Fields" old-time New York variety show included.

Occasionally there is a dog that is practically a coon exterminator, if he is hunting alone. He keeps his mouth shut, and sneaks along as stealthily as a wolf until he is almost on top of the coon, and either takes him, or pins him so close that he will go up the nearest tree at hand. Then he opens his mouth to tell you to come and get him. It takes a rather oversized, speedy, and brainy dog that can whip a coon at once, either on land or in the water, to fill the bill. For those that want this kind of a dog, he is the kind that fools the old wise coons, that has the habit of slipping in the closest ledge of rocks at the sound of the musical trailer. The silent trailer should not be allowed to hunt the coon. He is a fur dog, not a fun dog, and he spoils a lot of the latter. But you have got to hand it to him, when it comes to gathering coons, and who can dictate to a man what kind of coon dog he must keep? Probably the most efficient one of these dogs that ever hunted in this section was, according to looks, a cross between an English setter and a coach dog. He was picked up when a young pup, on the streets of New York—a typical mongrel! And then they will tell you that "no animal ever amounts to anything unless that animal is bred from a strain." I wonder what strains George Washington and Abe Lincoln were bred from? Is not the whole human race mongrels?

Many odd things happen on coon hunts. Here is one: A coon that was hard pinched scrapping with the dogs on the ground, jumped up on one of the fellows that was taking in the scrap, and then the dogs jumped up also, and down went the whole bunch. The fellow was yelling for all he was worth, but stopped all of a sudden. When the melee was over, someone asked him why he didn't keep on yelling, and he said, "I couldn't. One of the dogs had his foot in my mouth."

Yes, you can eat a coon, if you cut under the foreleg, and press over the shoulder blade from the body, and then cut out a nasty looking gland called the "strong" after you have done the rest of the dressing. They have an oily, ground taste, like a woodchuck, and the woodchuck has this gland, also. But the chuck is hardly worth mentioning, he is only a bag of intestines, anyhow. And when you have cleaned him, the little flesh you have left is only fit for some dog to eat that has no respect for himself. The coon, however, has quite some quantity of flesh, if you can stand the quality.

The passenger pigeon was never a sporting proposition, except for those that could not shoot on the wing. They hid at some feeding place and shot a bunch now and then. It might be white oak acorns, buckwheat, poke berries, or some other kind of food that the pigeon liked. This would only last for a day or so, except where there were large white oak trees in quantity on the edge of a swamp, and then they might stick around a week or so. Except very rarely, there were no shots to be had at a single pigeon on the wing. They were of a different nature than doves that make good wing shooting in some western states. Sometimes a flock of pigeons would fly over in reach of the gun when all one had to do was to stick the gun up in the air and pull the trigger. It didn't make any difference whether the gun was at your shoulder or not. The pigeons would begin to fall out of the flock, or slant down now and then as far as the eye could see. Half a dozen was about the average number retrieved. There were only a few breechloaders used to shoot pigeons. The first breechloader to show up in this country in the seventies was a pin fire from France, and there maybe weren't more than a dozen that were used to shoot pigeons. They were a dangerous gun, and their use soon died out, and before the safe breechloaders came out, the pigeons were practically gone. In the beginning, the old flintlock, the single-barrel "Twenty Shilling gun," the Springfield, the Queen Anne smooth bore musket, and the ten- and twelve-dollar guns—all muzzleloaders—shot about all the pigeons that were shot. There weren't many guns of any kind compared to now, and some of them were a joke.

One time a fellow saw a single pigeon on a dry tree and thought he would take a crack at him with the old flintlock. He sneaked along carefully until he came to a rail fence that was in range of the tree. The pigeon was wise to him, and was twitching her head around, as they always do when they get nervous. Well, he succeeded in getting the old gun on the top rail, took aim, and let her go! It made a click—woosh—BANG! At the click, the bird started, at the woosh, she was ten feet away from where she sat, and when the BANG came, she was at least twenty-five feet away. He might as well have shot in the opposite direction.

There was a special kind of long gun, however, that was used sometimes for shooting pigeons, with number seven shot, that had a very long barrel. The standard lengths were from thirty-six to forty inches, but these long ones were from fifty to seventy-two inches, and were used to kill sitting hawks, geese, ducks, etc., at extreme long range. They were twelve-bore and generally loaded with fifty (one ounce) of BB shot and four drams of good black powder. The powder pressure pushed the shot so long that they were accelerated to a far greater extent than they would have been from a short barrel, and when they left the muzzle they were traveling right along, and as a lot more energy was taken from the powder, the muzzle blast and report was much decreased, and the shot not separated by a high gas pressure from the rear after leaving the muzzle. These very long guns, though not choked, would hold the shot together better than the best choke bores of today. They got breech burnt like all muzzleloaders. Some were shortened for wing shooting, and they are gone. Magnum bores that shoot two ounces of BB shot will not put as many on the side of a duck at a hundred yards as one of these longest guns will with one ounce, and with nearly twice the penetration. The two-ounce gun will make a much larger pattern but nowhere near as dense. They use number two shot mostly, and they cannot get the killing effect necessary beyond eighty yards because the smaller the shot, the quicker the velocity is lost, the air-bucking surface being increased in proportion to weight. These guns were very unwieldy, and although they had a fin soldered on the underside of the barrel for stiffening, it was easily bent if someone fell down with it. The barrel was "swaybacked," to allow for the drop of a shot at long range. If a line was drawn from the top of the muzzle to the top of the breech, it would not touch the top of the barrel in the middle by maybe an eighth of an inch. If you shot about straight up at something, and did not see all the mark above the muzzle, most—if not all—the shot would pass between you and the mark. In other words, you would overshoot. Whether these long guns were made by individuals in this country, or at some foreign factory, is a question. They certainly were a wicked thing in a flock of sitting geese or ducks. At twenty rods they would put BB shot through a duck and lodge under the skin on the far side, and that is one hundred and ten yards. They served their purpose well on stationary targets.

When big business wants anything, they create a public sentiment that gets it. It is easier to make the other extreme, viz, a short-barrel gun, and if they can keep the wool pulled over the public's eyes, it will sell for just as much as a longer one, and that is all there is to the short-barrel stuff. It is just as easy to handle a forty-inch single barrel as it is a thirty-inch double, if the forty-inch gun is balanced, and that is not hard to do. All right, choose a thirty-six inch if you want to. Fred Kimbal killed more ducks on the wing with a gun that length than any man that has ever lived, and there has been some of the best partridge shooting done with one. Anything less than thirty-two inch simply does not give punch enough to the shot. A gun that does not put the shot through the bird to at least the skin on the far side at the maximum distance that a bird should be fired at, should not be allowed in the woods. Knocking off a handful of feathers and pricking the skin enough for gangrene to set in and kill the bird later on, is poor conservation. Partridges are susceptible to it.

If you won't use a long barrel, use one as long as you can, and don't load with a handful of shot and a pinch of powder. I know, fewer shot and more powder will make higher speed and a more open pattern, but better put one or two shot right through and pick up your bird, than to hit her with a handful and let her fly off to die. Do you know that the old-time market hunters used only one ounce of shot and from three and a half to five drams of powder? I wonder why our cannons have a barrel forty-some-odd feet long, and that "Big Bertha" that the Germans fired on Paris with was 112 feet long?* At least, it was claimed to be. They will tell you that smokeless powder is all burned up in the first twenty inches of a shotgun, as if that were all the good there was in it. We will suppose it is. We will say in a forty-inch barrel, and we have four tons per square inch of gas pressure, at the muzzle we will still have two tons minus a fraction for a change in temperature, and minus a whole lot that has put energy in the shot, and that is what is wanted? Pressure, force, velocity, energy, power,

---

*Editor's note: Here Barger is undoubtedly referring to the "Paris Gun," which is often confused with Big Bertha. The Paris gun was 118 feet long. It was used to shell Paris at a range of 75 miles, and its shells were projected so high that they were the first man-made objects to reach the stratosphere. Source: Wikipedia.

movement, electricity, and many other things—any one of which is nothing but heat in another form. We get more heat in the shot in a long barrel, and then call it velocity. Learn to load shotgun ammunition and what acceleration is. Get out your old book on "Natural Philosophy," now called physics. Look it up, and then look in Noah Webster's dictionary and see where he says that "a gas is a heat engine." You can't have anything printed like this in a sporting journal, for the advertisers run the journals, and nothing will be printed that might make some of them take their advertisements out. The journals should be run so the reader's interests come first, but they are not. And I doubt if they ever will be, as long as there is a fool born every minute. One sees piece after piece published that lauds the short gun, sometimes as short as twenty-seven inches, and then a load of three drams of powder and one and one quarter ounces of shot for a twelve bore at thirty yards. Full half of the birds will get away. It is about time the conservation commission stopped the crippling combination from being used on game, and the game warden and other officers should have the power to put any man's shotgun in a machine rest and if it did not shoot to point of aim with the center of the pattern, it should be barred out, the shot number taken, and unless it is remedied by the factory, anyone caught hunting with it, fined. There are lots of gun owners who are working on the edge of the pattern, and don't know it. There will be enough cripples when the gun is what it ought to be.

It is a mystery why so much science is applied to loading the rifle by individuals, and the shotgun is loaded by gosh and by guess. There is only a part of the trap shooters who know just what their gun is doing. But those who do are going to beat the fellow who doesn't, even if he is as good, and maybe a better pointer. I have loaded most of my shotgun ammunition since long before smokeless powder was invented. Curtis and Harvey's number four grain was the best in black. The first smokeless was "Woods" and it did not amount to much; if it was loaded a short while, it lost its strength. Then came Shultz's, and if it is properly loaded in a shell that is long enough to do so, it is a powder that will shoot with any powder made today. E.C. was a kind that was good in some guns, and in some was poor. Where a short shell was used to get enough strength and have ample room for wadding, Dupont's was it! The dense powders, such as Walsrode, Ballistite, and Laflin & Rand do not appeal to me. They must all start off with a high pressure and temperature. That is the fault with bulk smokeless, but it has been tamed down a whole lot, though any of it takes a strong powder to properly fire it, and such a high pressure coming on the shot so suddenly before they can get through the cone, does not do them any good. One dram of Curtis and Harvey's black powder loaded in a shell with a black powder primer, the balance of powder being bulk smokeless, will give a very good pattern, and the smoke will not bother, as smokeless powder is a smoke burner to quite an extent.

Big business may want to kill you if you start in to load your own, but you may find out that imported gun of yours was a "pig in a bag" when you bought it, as well as to find out you had been loading it wrong. Maybe everything will all come out fine, and then again some kid may come along with one of those gas pipes from Sears Roebuck and beat you all hollow. I have seen it happen. Some double guns will throw the center of the pattern to the point of aim, with one barrel, and the other will be way off. I will leave you to your own misfortune. Go to it! May you be situated where you will have the space to do it. The only kind of empty paper shells you will be able to get will not be what they used to be. The best shell that was ever made in America was green colored, and of a very thick and tough paper, made by the M.M.C. Co., and called their "Expert." There were none to be had after 1899. They out-shot everything in sight, whether they were hand loaded or factory loaded. The paper ones of today are too flimsy to stand reloading. Buy new empties, and don't expect to load them more than once.

FISH—EELS

In the early spring, those living near enough to brooks flowing in or out of the lakes used to spear enough black suckers to have a few feeds when they were spawning. Now it is unlawful to use a spear, and the suckers are allowed to breed without hindrance, and suck up all the eggs of older fish that they can find, and as they do their dirty work at night, the other fish don't seem to be able to drive them away. The eggs that fall down between the gravel stones are about all that get a chance to hatch on the average fish bed, or nest, so it is sometimes called.

And eels! One can anchor in any of the lakes in fifteen feet of water or more and catch eels, if the fishing is done on or near the bottom. In the olden times there were lots of eel lines set, baited with cut-up sunfish, and there were lots of eels caught for food. And even though there was never a game fish caught on this outfit, or in an eel pot, both were declared unlawful, and the eels are breeding to their hearts' content, and scrapping with the suckers over the eggs or maybe a black bass bed. There is also proof that eels sometimes have eaten eggs off a black bass bed in the daytime, and the bass though trying was unable to drive them off. Some used to get a can of bait stored in quiet waters, to use for fishing through the ice in winter, but that is unlawful now, as the brook where the bait must be caught is a trout brook, because a trout or two were caught in it fifteen or twenty years ago, that were put in it by someone who should have known that the water was too warm for them to propagate in. The lines were set in the ice in such a way that they could not freeze fast, unless they were neglected for a day or two. After a mess of fish were taken, the lines were unbaited, and the hook and loose line were let go to the bottom, until another mess were wanted, when they were baited up again. There was many an old cannibal pickerel taken, with sometimes two or three small pickerel in his stomach.

When one of these old "dreadnaughts" was taken, it probably gave fifty others a chance to gain at least middle size before being caught by some fisherman. White and yellow perch sometimes made a smell in the kitchen, but they seem to have run out, or lack food. Now they are few and small. The small-mouthed black bass, after he has eaten fifty times his own weight of other fish, if you happen to hook him, will go places and tear around like a calf on a rope, jump over the fence a time or two—Hold on! I mean the boat!—and cause a lot of excitement. If the fisherman happens to win the scrap, he might better turn him loose in the lake again, for if he is put through the frying pan route to the table, he is a poor substitute for a catfish. His big-mouth relation, however, in the same lake is different. When he is hooked, he makes a stab here and a stab there, and then gives right up, comes to the top of the water and rides along with his mouth wide open, giving a good imitation of an old shoe being dragged in. Anyone wanting to get such action out of a big-mouth black bass must shove on the line now and then to help him out. Probably I should not have mentioned the small-mouth black bass as a food fish, for he has about ninety percent fun and ten percent food value. But I want to say that ole "line sides," the big mouth, is a fair to middling fish when he gets to where they say, "Come and get it."

GAME—QUAILS

There used to be plenty of quails around these old farms, and most of the farmers made what they called stick traps, and caught enough maybe twice each fall to have a feed. If there were more than a dozen in the trap, the rest were let go. About half of what were on the place were caught, and no more. There were none wounded, as would have been the case if a gun had been used, and the right quantity was got at once. Sometimes, during a hard winter, the quails would come and eat with the chickens. The sportsmen of today who cannot adjust themselves to changes will think it was a horrible slaughter to catch quails that way. If they had been going to circumnavigate the earth, they would have never used an old tub like Magellan did. They would have gone round in a flying machine. It was in the seventies, after the cheap double guns came out, that an odd farmer took a serious interest in wing shooting, and if he hunted more than one day a week, he was called a shiftless cuss. My own mother told me, "You will never amount to anything, for your head runs all to a gun." Judging from the number of hunting licenses that are being sold nowadays, there are a lot of others that never will amount to anything.

As soon as wing shooting became popular, the trapping of quail ceased, and the boys had fun for a while. But in 1881, there was a spitting of snow all one day, and just about dark it snowed very hard until about ten o'clock, and then turned to rain, and about one o'clock in the morning the rain stopped, and it suddenly grew very cold, and stayed cold for a week. There was about sixteen inches of snow, counting the ice on top. The crust was so hard that cows walked on it without breaking through. Now, quails always roost out in the open, in a circle, heads out and tails in. This is probably done so they can scatter, and keep from flying against one another if they are suddenly disturbed. Their greatest mistake is in allowing themselves to get snowed under, and taking a chance of getting out when they want to. This storm trapped them all, and there was never any of that kind of quail seen alive again. After a couple of years, the boys chipped in, and got some quails from Virginia. They were only about half the size of the quails that were killed by the storm, and they had different habits. Instead of rising up out of the brush, and then leveling off, they would dive right through. We called them bumblebees. They never did well, and it wasn't the sportsman's fault, either. Some of them, however, pulled through the blizzard of '88.

GAME—PIGEON

And now, we come to the bird that supplied the United States with tons of food—the wild passenger pigeon. It was as much the custom to take the shotgun in the buckwheat field as it was the sickle and the cradle, so as to get the makings of a pigeon potpie. When a flock was sighted that were headed for a feed of buckwheat, the tools were dropped, the old gun was grabbed up, and everybody hid as best they could, the one with the gun choosing a hide-out in shooting distance of the most likely place for the pigeons to light. Sometimes, things didn't work out according to calculations. But they generally got enough before the day was over. For, when the old "Queen Anne Musket" that was loaded with half a handful, more or less, of black powder and number seven shot let go into the flock, there were some pigeons to pick up, and sometimes whoever did the shooting had to pick himself up also. They were birds of peculiar habits. Outside of the breeding season, they used to have a pigeon convention now and then. Apparently, all the pigeons in North America would get together in one, or not more than two, flocks, and after flying over the country for a day or two, they would break up in rather small flocks, and disperse again. Sometimes when this breaking up occurred, each flock would start for the Atlantic Ocean. It seems there was something on the beach that they fed on now and then. When this occurred, people living near the Atlantic coast could see pigeons flying from west to east all day long. Sometimes, there would be three or four flocks in sight at one time. It is history that one of these gigantic flocks was three miles wide, five miles long, and twenty feet deep. I have seen flocks myself that darkened the sun for a considerable length of time and made such a roaring that no one could talk without hollering in each other's ears.

They had another peculiar habit. They would light on some tree, and then light on top of each other, until their combined weight would bend the top of the tree over to the ground, if it was a small one, or the limbs of a large tree, and sometimes a limb, or the tree, would break. If this wasn't a devilish prank, what was it?

It is claimed by many people that these birds were all shot off. To any close observer with the benefit of firsthand knowledge, this is a fallacy. One year there were millions, and the next there were practically none. The gun could not have done this. Shortly after the main bulk was missing, it was published in some paper that a ship traveling north at a point about five hundred miles south of the Gulf of Mexico went through dead pigeons for miles, that were floating on the ocean. This flock no doubt got lost in a fog and drowned, after flying until they were exhausted. And it was published in another paper that a schooner off the coast out from Nantucket was caught in a fog, and after laying at anchor all night, pigeons began lighting on the vessel, evidently being attracted by the sound. All that could get a footing, did so, and soon they were lighting on each other, and finally bunches would fall off here and there, as near as could be ascertained from inside the cabin, and the crew claimed that is all that saved the vessel from sinking. In about forty-eight hours, the fog lifted and those that were on the schooner apparently made it to land. But the ocean was covered with dead pigeons as far as the eye could see in any direction, and they weren't very scattered either. The article went on to say that they washed ashore in Nantucket Bay, and the poor people picked them for their feathers, until they were too much decayed. The remnant that was left probably flew themselves to death, or to at least a nonbreeding condition, looking for the main flocks, as they had a strong gregarious nature. It may be that they were like some other species, that after being reduced to a small number, will go on down and out, in spite of all that men can do. The heath hen of Martha's Vineyard is a good example of that. According to fossil evidence, nature has wiped out a vast number of species since life began. But we only make a fuss over those that pass out during or near our lifetime.

It was the robbing of the squabs from the pigeons' nests that caused their extermination. They were no doubt looking for a part of the world where they would not have their nests molested when they were drowned at sea in a fog. Their main rookery, or breeding place, was in the Kankakee swamp. Their nests were robbed and tons of squabs sent to Chicago and other places. There was no artificial refrigeration in those days, and the major portion spoiled. When the market was glutted, sometimes barrels of squabs would be rolled out on the sidewalk with tags on them stating, "15 cents for the barrel, squabs and all." The newspapers were full of this at the time. There were no records kept in those days of such things as pigeons and the like, that were considered of minor importance.

Indeed, they did not record births and deaths of people in many, if any places, at that time, except perhaps in the Bible, or the almanac, and if they were lost, it was just too bad for anybody that cared in after years when they were born. I know some people right now in the year of our Lord 1939 that would give a considerable sum to know for sure what year they were born in.

Whatever the cause of their demise, the passenger pigeons are gone forever, and the man on the rocky farm felt their loss the most. Several of them said, "The old home has never been the same since those swift and graceful birds left the sky—and the dinner pot."

Editor's note: The following handwritten section of one of Barger's letters to his daughter Flossie was included in the microfilm version housed at the New York State Library.

The National Geographic Society's Journal for Aug. 1939 prints in a write up of the State of Iowa an item about the passenger pigeon thus (White Pine Hollow, between Dubuque and Guttenberg, containing all that is left of the once magnificent forest which helped feed sawmills of the river cities.

In early times migrating passenger pigeons flew over this woodland in such numbers that *they darkened the sky for days.* Slaughter of thousands of them by settlers seemed not to diminish flocks. But in 1871 the main body went north never to return. A few of this now extinct species were seen in Iowa as late as 1876).

This shows they know nothing definite, and are writing any old thing. There were millions up to some time around the middle 70's when they suddenly disappeared, except a few stragglers. I shot my last one in the early eighties, out of a flock of seven. As far as I know that was about the last of them although you can read now a days any old thing about them.

The following is from a letter from Barger to his daughter:

Now about this pigeon stuff: I have been thinking hard as I can, and now it appears to me that I saw one of the pieces about drowning in a fog in the "Sun" and the editor at that time was Chas. L. Dana. All the articles I read said the Kankakee swamp rookery was practically the whole cheese so far as a breeding place for pigeons was concerned. It is south of Chi. And I think in Indiana.

Now I have been digging in the back numbers of the National Geographic Soc. Journals and I found a lot, some of which I think is silly. The hordes of these birds were reduced about ninety nine percent in one year so far as the section I was in indicated, and from reading and hearing it was so all over.

Now I want to call your attention to something before quoting some of the things the Geographic says. I can't give you all without writing half a day. You can read it when you come on.

When the old birds were breeding, they were thin and tough, and hardly fit for eating, and never was eaten so far as I know. They fed the squabs from the milk glands in the throat, and both parents done this. Now it was the *squabs* that had a market value. Even in the fall of the year a while after the breeding season had been over for several weeks the old birds were thinner and tougher than the young birds, and at this season of the year there was a very small percentage that reached market. They were consumed locally, and these birds were taken with the gun, but the amount was only fractional to that of the squabs taken from the nest. For the adult birds knew how to take care of themselves to quite an extent. It is true there were quite a number taken in nets, but the amount has been grossly exaggerated.

This talk about the gun being used at the breeding places is all tommy rot. Powder and shot cost money, and if it didn't what would be the use of shooting squabs in the nest, and have to go up the tree anyhow to get them, or maybe punch them out with a pole or cut the tree down?

This claiming that the passenger pigeon was extermi- nated by shooting the squabs and the old ones at the nest is the dumbest thing that was ever put in print.

And now for some of the things the "Geographic" says. "A century ago the great naturalist James Audubon observed this species in such abundance that he did not believe its numbers would ever be greatly diminished." Mr. Kalm "wrote of a flock that he observed in flight in Pennsylvania in March 1740 that was three to four miles in length, and a mile in breadth. A more graphic description is that of Alexander Wilson, who told of great columns of the birds eight or ten miles in length, and of flocks extending across the sky, whose steady procession continued for more than an hour. The passing of these multitudes was said to darken the sun like the sudden coming of a storm cloud, and the steady sound of their myriads of beating wings was likened to the roar of a waterfall."

"Alexander Wilson reports a nesting colony near Shelbyville, Kentucky, that covered an area a mile wide, and more than *thirty miles long [emphasis added]*. S.S. Stevens described to William Brewster a nesting near Petoskey Michigan in 1876 or 1877 that, with an average width of three or four miles, extended *28 miles*. It was not unusual to see a hundred nests in a tree, and the heavy-bodied birds often crowded in desirable groves until large limbs were broken by their weight. The ground in their colonies was strewn always with fallen nests, eggs, and young, and was covered with the droppings of the multitude of birds."

"Gunpowder gave greater killing power than sticks or arrows and there was a sale for pigeons in the markets. . . . Men with axes cut down the nest-laden trees to obtain the heavy squabs. Others with long poles knocked the helpless nestlings to the ground. Netters operated continuously with spring nets to capture adults by the score. For decoys live birds with their eyelids sewn together were fastened on movable perches. When flying flocks appeared, the decoys were set in motion and their flapping wings called their passing companions down to destruction." (This last quotation shows total ignorance of the way a stool pigeon was used, and one that couldn't see good was of no use whatever. My uncle Alfred Crawford had one and used to catch some now and then. I was with him twice I think in the 'bow house' and saw the whole operation, will explain to you sometime)

"In 1879 Pro. H.B. Roney estimated that 5,000 men were engaged regularly in pigeon hunting as a business."

"One account says 990,000 dozen pigeons were shipped in three years from western Michigan to New York City. Another tells of three carloads per day, each car load containing 150 barrels of pigeons, shipped from one town for forty days. The birds sold for from twenty cents a dozen upward. Roney reports shipment of one and one half million birds from Petoskey Michigan, between March 22 and Aug. 12, 1878. In addition more than 80,000 birds were shipped alive for use in trap shooting" (There were only a limited number of wild birds used for this purpose. Trap shooting was in its infancy).

"The passenger pigeon fed on nuts seeds and berries" (This is only a part of their food, it was acorns and buckwheat mostly).

"There are many stories of the Passenger pigeon having migrated en masse to unknown forests in South America, but in more than a hundred years of investigation naturalists have never had record of this bird beyond Cuba and central Mexico."

(How could they get a record of their being in South America if they got drowned in a fog trying to get there)?

I can see now that it must have been later than 1878 that I read what I did, about the ship sailing through dead pigeons.

In those days there was a good many "Reporters Dreams" as they were called. Just a lot of lies to fill up space. Just the same there were some things taken for lies that were the truth, and I believe the one about the floating dead pigeons was one of them. You can see from what I have given you from the Geographic that they are like a drowning man grappling at a straw.

I don't know how old the Geographic is, nor the Audubon Society, but it is plain they have no authentic detailed record of what became of the Passenger pigeon, any more than I have. And probably not as much for they failed to read what I did, or else have forgotten it.

However I have learned from them how to handle the situation if the pigeons ever come back again.

First put two cents worth of ammunition in your gun, and with it shoot the squabs guts out. Then climb the tree and get him. Then send him to market and get a penny for him, provided the market isn't glutted, and he doesn't stink.

No wonder! them old timers made so much money.

GAME—SQUIRRELS AND RABBITS

Gray squirrels were used as food to a limited extent, generally taken by use of a treeing dog and a shotgun, so as to get enough for a "mess" (a mess means enough for one full meal for the family) at one time, and not have two or three hanging up getting unfit to eat, waiting for more. And rabbits. They were always a standby, until a few years back when they and the squirrels were both taken away because of an infernal disease called "tularemia." Whoever handles the flesh is liable to get infected, and either die or become invalid for life. It is foolish to take a chance. It is impossible to tell the infected ones from the others, except when they are pretty far gone with the disease. They tell you that after being cooked they are harmless, but who wants to eat a diseased animal, except perhaps the Gypsies? So, the people on the rocky farm can also strike Brer Rabbit off their bill of fare.

GAME—PARTRIDGE

The woods have quite a few partridges in them yet, probably ten per cent of what there used to be, and no doubt there would be several times more than there are if it wasn't for the gluttonous robins.

They have increased by leaps and bounds. They flock up in the fall of the year, and they are the most gluttonous birds there are. They eat everything in sight as clean as a whistle before they go south, so that the partridge needs to get in good condition so as to pull through the winter. In fact, some foods that the robins eat could be reached by the partridge when a deep snow is on the ground, such as frost grapes, where the vines have climbed way up in the trees. And then, these robins when they get south are a pest at the rice fields, and they are called rice birds there. They shoot a lot, trying to protect the rice, and if I am rightly informed, one can get them served up for twenty-five cents in most any of the eating places.

There is many a lady that thinks more of a robin red breast on the lawn than she does of all the partridges on earth, and there is many a sportsman that thinks more of a partridge than he does of all the robins on earth, and they both have a right to their opinion. Partridges are food for a limited few, for while most anybody can shoot a partridge, it isn't everybody that can pick one up.

GAME—WOODCHUCK

Where was the woodchuck when Columbus discovered America? It was all woods then, was it not? Is that why they got the name of woodchuck? Did the first settlers chuck one in the pot now and then? Do you know that to this day there are quite a few wood-chucks that live in the big woods, where there is no grass, and eat acorns, roots, and other mast like a squirrel? And do you know that they feed nights, and can climb to the very top of the tallest trees, and when coon hunting was done earlier in the season than is allowed now, and before the chucks holed up for the winter, that the coon hunters used to shoot one occasionally, that the dog treed, when the dog happened to get between him and his hole before being discovered? They are very dark, and some are jet black. They appear to be odd ones that have never taken to the open farms. Some are a mile or more from any open ground.

A lazy boy would have him a woodchuck, that he thought would chuck his wood, but he would not give the woodchuck his chuck, so the woodchuck wouldn't chuck his wood! And here is a recipe, if you want to cook a woodchuck: After cleaning, taking the strong out, and salting, wrap him in three or four thicknesses of damp cheesecloth, and have some clean blue clay, that you have taken from where some brook has uncovered it, mix it with a liberal portion of finely chopped onions, adding enough sweet milk to make it the consistency of stiff dough. Put an even coating of this over the cheesecloth that is on the woodchuck, about two inches thick, and wrap the whole thing with some more clean cloth. Put it into a regular dripping pan, and bake in a medium hot oven for about two hours. When you open it up, throw away the woodchuck, and eat the milk, onion and clay mixture. But, if you have forgotten to take out the "strong," none of it will be fit to eat, and in that case, you better throw the dripping pan away, for you might want to cook a skunk in it sometime, and it would taint the skunk.

GAME—SKUNK

And now that a skunk has been mentioned, a little about him may not be amiss. At one time some of the farmers set stone traps on a flat rock for skunks, and when the stone fell, the skunk's brain was smashed so quick he would not throw his scent. Then, by working carefully, the outlet could be tied off, and the scent glands skinned out and thrown away, or put in a bottle to sell. After the glands are off the job, the skunk can be skinned without any more smell than there is in skinning a rabbit. Skunk's oil is colorless, odorless, and tasteless, if gotten out of the skunk in the right way, and it used to sell for five dollars a gallon, and was used for those persistent, hanging-on colds that one sometimes gets. It retailed in the drugstore for one dollar an ounce, and probably does yet, or for more. It is the most penetrating oil known. It comes out through the skin when taken internally, and goes in through the skin when rubbed in for rheumatism. If the merest speck of the scent gets in the oil, it is ruined for internal use. If skinned as above, and the whole carcass laid on some wooden sticks that are put across the top of a glass dripping pan, and put in the oven with the oven door part open, all the oil will come out of the skunk. No metal should come in contact with the oil, and it must not be overheated, or it will turn straw color, and will not be saleable.

One time some folks were sitting in the kitchen having a glass of hard cider now and then, and there was one of these skunks getting his oil tried out in the oven, and it smelled as good as a turkey. One of the party said, "If I had another glass or two of cider in me, I believe I would try a piece of him."

Along about sixty years ago a fellow was trying to skin out the scent glands in an odorless manner, but he let his knife slip, and punctured one, and so far as the skinner of that skunk knows, what is left of him is right there in that spot yet! Sticking the blade in the ground about a dozen times and smelling of it, didn't wholly remove the odor.

A skunk is a bad actor in a hencoop, though not as bad as a mink. They kill more than they can eat sometimes. One night there was a commotion in the henhouse, and the farmer went to see what was up. When he opened the door, whew! He found out, all right. His wife yelled, "What is it?" He said, "A skunk," and she said, "Did he get any chickens?" He said, "I guess so, and he can have the rest for all of me, I have got enough!"

There is a minute quantity of skunk scent mixed with perfumes to act as a binder. It makes it far more durable. It sure is one devilish substance. It hangs on so. If a dog has killed a skunk two months before, if he gets wet and comes in the house, you will have to drive him out, or get out yourself. Dampness brings it out, but a dry heat will finally get the best of it, maybe by the time you are gray headed. If a skunk can get a little of it in a dog's eyes, the dog will be out of commission for some time. He will turn on his back and squirm along like a snake trying to rub it out of his eyes, and then when he gets on his feet, he will vomit up everything but his tail. People who have had it in their eyes say it pains the same as though cayenne pepper was thrown in their eyes.

The skunk seems to be able to deodorize himself quickly, for there is never any smell around the mouth of his den, unless someone makes a steel trap there, and gets one of its inmates, and then the rest will leave. There is sometimes a dozen or two in the den during the fur season. This has been found out in three different ways, by catching them near the den, by tracking them in light snow when the weather is warm enough for them to travel, and by being dug out by those who can stomach a smell. Though it doesn't seem to be as virulent in cold weather, and they being dumpish are not so quick to squirt their "dyestuff." As soon as a head shows up, a twenty-two bullet through the brain prevents the turning of the other end. Sometimes a whole denful is taken without anyone getting "touched up." Those that have their dens in rock ledges are safe from "Johnny dig 'em out." But during the World War when fur was so high, the earth dens were probably all cleaned out. A skunk skin that is about half white sells for most nothing, a broad stripe for a little more, a short stripe for more yet, and the "star" that has a white spot in his face, a little white maybe between the shoulders and some white on the end of his tail, sells for top price. And if this top price is five dollars, the half white skunk will be worth about fifty cents. Now, all these skins are dyed, and fetch up together in Madam's "Russian Sable" coat. If the texture of the fur of the white skunk is better than the black one, it will be the better fur after dyeing. I suppose it is natural that there should be some skinning done in the skin business. In the beginning, before dyeing was done, the black fur was all that was used, and of course was worth more. If custom suits big business, it will be the same as it was in Grandpop's time. If not, it has been busted up long ago. That is why they weigh potatoes and weigh eggs.

SNAKES

Whoever heard of a farm that didn't have some snakes on it? We will start with rattlers. In the last fifty years, there have been two killed that were bona-fide rattlesnakes, and were both killed not far inland from the Hudson River, though several years apart. It is a poor ad for a man's place if he wants to sell it to let it be known that there has been a rattlesnake killed on it. There are no doubt more rattlers and especially copperhead snakes (called chunk heads) than the people dream about, for they are mostly nocturnal. The pupils of their eyes are nothing but a narrow vertical slit in the daytime, but in the nighttime they are round, on the same principle of cats' eyes, and if a lantern light is thrown on them, they look like two round coals of fire, and look much bigger than they are. They are enough to give a dead man a start, and they smell like cucumber vines in the nighttime. I am speaking of the copperhead, and in warm weather when they are out after their food, they lay out in the sun in the early spring, and late fall, and in very dry weather they resort to wet meadows, and keep under the long grass where it is cool, and that is why they are found now and then, when the grass is getting mowed. No doubt, the coon hunters would run on them oftener than they do when the woods are part wet if it wasn't that the cold weather has made them crawl in where it is warmer.

One lady got bit with a copperhead a long time ago, when she was seeding out her flower garden in a dry time, the garden being irrigated at the time. The heat had driven him down off the mountain to where it was cool. She had quite a time of it, out of her head, and so on, but she lived through it. She went part blind, and part deaf, after it, and she laid it to the snake bite. And maybe it did cause it, for a dog got bit a few years after that, and he went deaf and nearly blind, and had to be shot.

And now we come to harmless (?) snakes. Take a black snake, for instance. He will spiral around a tree, and go up in a jiffy. Then he putters around a bird's nest, and tries to grab the old one, and does quite often. If he don't he will get outside of the eggs, or young ones, and a nest of partridge eggs or a brood of young ones are just his pie. He sometimes swallows a garter snake, if he is rather hungry. I will say, there is one thing he is good for—if you can catch one, and a water snake about the same size, and throw them down on the floor that has had some sand put on it so they can't get a grip to run away, you will see one of the swiftest scraps of your life. A part of the time they are in a "ball of blurs," as one fellow described it.

If you put a trout in a spring, a black snake will go in the spring and roil it all up, and as the trout can't live in roily water long, he will come to the top and the snake will take him. Where did he learn that a trout cannot stand very roily water? He sure must be one of the devil's imps. "As wise as a serpent" is a saying handed down, and I believe a black snake can reason. They sometimes shake their tail in a bunch of dry leaves. Now, if they are not trying to make you think they are a rattlesnake, what are they doing? They will rise right up more than half their length sometimes, and come right at you, and if you stand your ground they will stop about ten feet from you and siss like a goose, and stick their tongues out, while weaving their head from side to side. If they can bluff you out, that is what they want. They will chase you if you run, but if you go right at them, you will have to run like a greyhound to catch one.

I was hunting one time, and happened to stop for a little while to listen to something. All of a sudden, I heard the leaves rattle about twenty feet away. I looked and saw a chipmunk come out from under a flat stone that was resting on some smaller stones. The rock was about ten feet across. The chipmunk was in such a hurry I thought there was another one following him, and that they were playing, but it was a blacksnake that was after him. The chipmunk knew he could not outrun the snake, so he tried to duck him, by running around and going under the other side of the same stone. In about a second, here they came again, and did exactly the same thing over again. Yes, and here they came a third time. But the blacksnake reversed, and ran in where he had come out of, and I never saw either of them after. It was plain to me that he met the chipmunk coming from the other way, and nabbed him. That taught me two things: that a blacksnake can reason, and that he can't make much speed going around a curve.

One time a fellow was raising trout and he noticed some garter snakes around the pond, and thought they were after frogs. One day he noticed a movement in the water nearby, and he saw a garter snake with a live young trout in his mouth, about three inches long. He came out of the water and swallowed it. When the snake was killed and cut open, he had three young trout in him.

One day, the lady of the house and the children heard a commotion around the fowl in the dooryard. The old rooster was slamming at something, and the old hen was pecking at something in the grass, and all the little chickens were peeping for all they were worth. Come to find a rather large-sized garter snake had hold of a little chicken. Say, what is a harmless snake? I can tell you, that one was, after the kids got through with him. The little green snake that can run on the tops of tall grass, making each spear hold up a little of his weight, is harmless. So is a hognosed adder. He makes himself look like a cobra, and plays dead if you touch him. A milk snake is good to have around to catch mice, but he will drink his fill of milk, if he can get at it. There are a very few black adders, and they will bite a stick, if you crotch one down, but they are not supposed to be poisonous. But have a care, for once in a blue moon, there is a black copperhead. There was a fellow that just missed getting hit by a hair, that made this mistake. There are light cream-colored copperheads, iron rust color, jet black, and many shades between, and more of them than we know about. When the Bear Mountain Bridge approach was blasted out, they killed a few. If you run into a copperhead, he will stay put, as long as you are looking at him, but if you turn your back to get a stick or something, when you come back he will be gone.

It is peculiar that nearly all kinds of snakes den up together in the winter. If you know where there is a snake den, and go the first sunshiny day of spring, you may see half a bushel of snakes, copperheads and all, out sunning themselves. Green snakes, water-snakes, and rattlers excepted. At least, that has been my experience. As soon as they get over their dumpishness, and the weather warms up a little, they will scatter. They may come out and go back again in several odd days before this happens.

VARIOUS ANIMALS

The old she fox is the greatest offender in killing young partridges. She has her young to feed at the same season of the year that the partridge does, and if she locates a flock of young chicks, none escape, for she can smell them out the same as a setter or a pointer dog. I have seen an old she fox kill a whole brood of chicks before

I realized what she was doing. I thought she was catching frogs, until the old partridge flew up after she knew that the last one was killed. It was on a piece of wet meadow land, adjacent to the woods. The grass and weeds were about eight inches high. It was only about three hundred yards from the house, and I could see her stand still for quite a little while, and then make a dive, and get something in her mouth, that she took over to the foot of a bush at the edge of the meadow, and then go right back again, to smell out another one. When it was all over, she went to the bush and gathered the chicks in her mouth, and went away.

Sometimes bird dogs get a notion to hunt chicks this time of year, and kill and eat a lot. A red squirrel will bite the intestines out of the chicks, with the old one flying at him, but he is too quick for her. He does not eat any part, but does it out of pure cussedness. The same as when he cuts off green pears and other fruit that he has no earthly use for. He is so quick the devil couldn't catch him, and that is how he escaped from Hades. It has been stated that there was once a tree and lightning struck it. He beat the lightning all the way to the ground, jumped off, and never got touched.

There was a mare that would jump on a double stone wall, and then jump down on the other side. You could turn her in the garden, and she wouldn't touch a thing. Nor would she take a bite of clover if you turned her in where it was half way up to her eyes, but as soon as you turned your back, she would jump over the fence, and go picking around and be satisfied, even if it was on a stubble. She would never trot when you were on her back. It was either walk or run, and she would never run in harness. Sometimes, when she was in double harness, and she let out on her trotting, her mate would have to run to keep up, and they looked funny enough to make a dog laugh. They appeared to be trying to shake the harness off, and everything all to pieces, clear to the tailboards of the wagon.

There was a monstrous overgrown hog on one place that used to eat just all he could hold, and then bite and root all the other hogs away from the trough so they couldn't get anything. The way he took care of that swill! It looked as though he thought it was money, and that he intended to leave some libraries after him, or something. It is bad enough for some people to be that way, but a hog ought to know better.

A certain dog used to crawl around until he thought he could beat a woodchuck to his hole, and then he ran at the hole instead of the woodchuck. He would either drag or slat the chuck down the side hill so as to get him at a disadvantage, as he wasn't big enough to kill one without an extended scrap. On account of water flooding them out if they dig their holes on level ground, they most always dig them on a side hill, and generally under the lower side of a rock, and that trait was the undoing of many a chuck, for this dog would size up the situation from a distance, and when the chuck was feeding a considerable distance from the hole, the dog would go way off around, and sneak up to the opposite side of the rock, and by running around the rock again, the chuck was caught off his guard.

VIII

COUNTRY STORE
AND ELECTION

COUNTRY STORE

The storekeeper used to get his molasses by the hogshead (sixty-three gallons) and sell it by the gallon to all who came after it with jugs. It took considerable time to dispose of that much, but finally when the last of the molasses ran out there would be anywhere from ten to twenty-five pounds of molasses sugar left in. There used to be bids made for the hogshead before the molasses was out, so as to get the two large tubs that the hogshead would make after sawing it in two, and also to get the sugar. The tubs were used to mix feed in for the cattle, for watering troughs, bait fish cans, and other purposes, and the sugar tasted about as good as maple sugar.

Well, the fellow that made the highest bid and got the hogshead one spring let it be known to a few of his friends that he was going to open it on a certain day, so they were on hand with their little tin pails to get some sugar. He started in the bunghole with a compass saw, until he could get a regular carpenter's saw in the cut, and at it he went. It is a long way around a hogshead, and the staves are thick and of oak. He would saw a while, and rest a while. After he had perspired plenty, and was tired, he had some three feet or more left to saw on the bottom. The saw commenced to jump and jump. He said there was a big splinter split loose, that was pinching the saw, and that he did not like to roll the hogshead around, as it would make the mixture of the sawdust with the sugar worse. Well, he kept on with the saw jumping until he got almost through, when the jumping stopped, and he soon finished, and dumped the two halves on their heads. He looked in, and he had haggled an alligator in two in the middle that was about two and a half feet long. We forgot all about wanting any sugar, and left the man looking in the tub. When I got home my father asked me why I didn't have any sugar, and when I told him the reason he had a good laugh, but all of a sudden his face straightened up, and he said, "Dammit, I have been eating the molasses off that alligator all winter."

A big gawky young fellow of some six feet came in the store one day, rolled his eyes around, let on what a big time he was going to have, said he had been savin' up about six months to go to the Fair, had a'most four dollars, and was going to spend every cent, and then walked over and got him a handful of butter crackers and a piece of cheese, and later on a "chaw o' tobaccur" out of the pail. All three of these articles were given out gratuitously. The tobacco came in very large-sized pails, and was called "weigh out tobacco." Some nicknamed it "way off tobaccur."

They used to wear coats with a split tail, and on each side of the split tail on the inside, there was a pocket. Most everybody had a muzzleloading shotgun of some sort, and in the average loading a quarter pound of powder would go as far as a pound of shot. An old fellow came in and ordered these two articles. The shot was weighed out of a sack, and the powder out of a ten-pound keg on the regular counter scales. The lead powder plug was screwed back in the keg, and the very last grain of loose powder dumped off the head of the keg for safety sake, and the keg put way back in the end of the store in the corner, as was the usual custom. He put the shot in one coattail pocket, and the powder in the other. After, he was gabbing away with his old cronies for a half hour or so, he put his old pipe, not thinking, in the pocket with the powder, and WHOOP! The place was so full of smoke everybody was cackling and couldn't see. Someone happened to be near the door, and yanked it open or they might have suffocated before they could get out. They crawled out on their hands and knees as it was. If the keg had gone up, it would have been just too bad. They finally got the fire out on what was left of the old fellow's coattail, and nearby clothing, put some laudanum on where he got burned (as was the remedy for most anything in those days), and had a few glasses of hard cider all around, and they were ready for coon stories again.

Someone went and got an old "sojercoat" that was made for the soldiers of the Civil War, and used as an everyday coat by many farmers when the weather or occasion called for it. This covered up the effects of the old fellow's mishap in getting home very nicely. A fellow passing the store when the powder went off said that he could see that the dogs had made up their minds instantly that it was no place for them. He said, "They came out like cannonballs, and lit clean across the road."

The general variety of conversation and actions between fox and coon stories ran something like this: "Zackarias' steers run away with him and his cart yistady. They were goin' like the wind when they went by my house. I hollered and ast him where he was goin'? And he hollered back, "How do I know?"

There was one of the neighbors that had an extremely long nose. And he had been baptized a week or so before in an enlarged and quiet part of the brook, that was suitable for it. One says to the other, did you see that feller get baptizes t'other day? Yes. Did the preacher shove him all the way under? Yes, and his nose went in a muskrat hole, and three or four run out.

One went to the door, and threw out an awful cud. Another one said, you better git the tate fork, and go out and spread that around a little, or nobody can git by. Did you hear about the feller that bought a hoss from a dealer and the hoss died right away? He went and told the dealer, and he said, he never done that when I had him.

The youngsters was pitching whatever they could get to make up a set, an old hoss shoe or two, a piece of bent iron, and so on. One had a piece of a hoss's shank. I asked him how he could use that, and he said, It's all right, it's got a ringbone on it.

Now it so happens that two or three miles back up in the hills where there is only garden spots, or very small farms, the people are several degrees nearer the primitive than are the people around the store, and they make fun of them, the same as the city people does of them. There were a few of these way back-in fellows that had so much hair on their faces, and around their eyes, that they looked like spitz dogs. There was only one person that I ever saw that had more hair on his face than one of them, and that was Barnum's Jojo, the dog-faced boy. Here is one of the store boys tell about them: Two of them met in the woods, and one raised his gun up. The other said, What are you going to do there? I always said that if I ever saw anyone that looked worse than I do, I would shoot him. The other one looked at him a while and said, If I do look any worse than you do, you can let her go!

One said he went out at dusk one evening and there was a flock of birds flying around that at first he took for whippoorwills, but they made so much noise he knew they couldn't be. He went in the house and got his old gun. It was so dark he had a hard time pintin' it, but he finally brought one down. When he took it in to the lamplight, it was nothing but one of a flock of misskeeters that had flew over from Jersey.

A friend came up to hunt, and one evening I took him over to the store. At first, the bunch was skittish of a fellow from the city, but after we bought two or three gallons of cider, and they got part lit, they loosened up. They got off a lot of jokes, most of which had been handed down from colonial days, but as he laughed at them all, they thought he had never heard them before. He was almost bursting over the way they got them off. He dare not let himself out too much, for fear they would tumble to what he was really laughing at, and shut up. He went outside now and then to try and get some of the laugh out of him, and then he would come in for another dose.

Going over the hills home, he would stop in the road every now and then and bend over with his arms across his stomach and laugh. He said his stomach hurt him awful every time he laughed, but he couldn't help it. I slept with him that night, and although we retired late, long before daylight the bed trembled so it woke me up, and it was him laughing again. And when he went away, he told me that if he could produce exactly on the stage what he had seen and heard in that store, his fortune would be made. Now this was many years before Denman Thompson brought out his play called "The Old Homestead."* In all probability, it was experiences of this kind that gave him his cue that city people will laugh themselves into fits over the ways and expressions of the backwoods country people.

There were two fellows that lived on charity. One had his hands and arms almost totally paralyzed, and the other one had one leg totally and the other partially paralyzed. There was great jealousy between them and every time they came together, they quarreled. They met at an election, and go to fighting. One struck, and the other kicked. The one that struck with his crutch was holding his own pretty good until finally, the one that kicked landed one on the shin bone of his opponent's best leg, and he went down as if he had been shot, and then being at a disadvantage, the crowd separated them. Some of the old-timers said that it was the most laughable fight they ever saw, or ever expected to see. The one that got kicked said, "I want to outlive him, if it is only for a day." And fate decried that it should be so. It wasn't many years after that, that the one that done the kicking died, and the very next day, the other one died.

ELECTION

The country store was quite an institution, one in particular that had a so-called town house across the road from it that was used as a polling place, and was the scene of some typical country sayings and actions, as well as those that were pulled off in and about the store surroundings. Sometimes on election day, there would be dog fights, man fights, a nearby ball game, plenty of hard cider a little way off, some of the trustees around behind the barn buying votes,

---

*Editor's note: The Old Homestead premiered in Boston in 1886.

and now and then some politician would jump up in the back end of a wagon and throw a handful of one-dollar bills to the winds, and holler, "Hurrah," for somebody. That was the candidate he was rooting for. Now, if there is any football team that can beat the scrabble that followed one of these money throwings, they would have to go some. Some gave themselves away that had been carrying around a crutch or a cane, by fighting harder than the rest. It was wonderful how quick some of them would lose their "rumatiz" that they had been "jes dyin'" with! There were busted suspenders, busted eyes, bloody noses, pulled-out whiskers, and many other casualties, after the fracas was over.

The town house was only big enough to hold a percentage of the crowd at a time, and the poll clerks had a tough time of it. First, one would come in and puff tobacco smoke as hard as he could, and stay in about as long as he could breathe, and then the next one, or the next bunch would do the same, until it got so thick they just had to open the windows, and then the papers would blow all around the place, and instead of the air being white from the smoke, it would turn blue from profanity. Those that chewed didn't do anything to interrupt proceedings, but they made some work for the fellow that owned the wagon underneath, for the tobacco juice went through the cracks in the floor, and spattered it aplenty.

"Hear ye, hear ye! The polls of this election will close in five minutes unless voters appear." After you heard this for the last of about six times being bawled out of the window, they would begin counting the votes, or "canvassing" as they called it, and it took until late at night to finish. One presidential election about ten thirty in the evening the democrats were way ahead and the canvassing was near through. A democrat rushed downstairs and out, and bawled out, "Just as I respected. Hancock's elected."

IX

Education, Religion,
and War

THE RED SCHOOLHOUSE

Every country schoolhouse with hardly any exceptions was a rectangular box about thirty to thirty-five feet long, including the entry, up to some thirty years ago, and sometimes these boxes held as high as sixty scholars. In the wintertime, some were being roasted near the old wood stove, and some were freezing to death way back in the corners. Sometimes they used to let them shift every half hour in bitter weather. If my fingers hadn't been frozen half the time, maybe I would have learned to write.

There were two long low benches that ran almost the length of the schoolroom proper, and were nearer the center on either side of the stove, and were for the little kids. Where they passed the stove they used to get so hot the pine gum would come oozing out of them. These seats had no back, nor rest in front. The books had to be held in the hand, or on the lap. Then there were two high seats that also ran the length of the room, without backs. But they did have a book rest, the same length, that was of a slant, and built integral with the "school box," there being a lip at the front to keep pens and pencils from rolling off. They say, "Pine is soft wood." Darned lie! If you had to sit on one of those benches for just one day, you would know better. You had to plug from nine in the morning until five in the evening, right under the teacher's eye, and you either got your lesson or you got something that made it more disagreeable to sit on those benches. Some scholars came from over a mile, and on foot—many times through those deep snows we used to have. It had to be more than knee deep to keep from going to school. Nowadays, there is a bus to come and get you, and bring you back again. Only in school a few minutes. They have a holiday for most everybody that ever died, except those of the Smith family, and at the drop of a hat, they will declare a week's vacation. It is disgusting to us old-timers to see what we have missed: a Jim Dandy gymnasium to play in and all!

The old schoolhouse is RED because of a Chinese paint that was many times more durable than any paint that is known to science, and what has become of it is a mystery. It was cheap paint, and granaries, barns, and schoolhouses were all painted with it, as well as many a boat. Right now, there are places where that paint has been on for nearly eighty years, without any other paint or anything being put over it, and the wood is as sound under it as the day it was put on, and it is right out in the weather. Blowing sand and hail will wear it off where it is exposed to them, but it will last almost indefinitely under ordinary exposure. Maybe it is kept out of the country so there will be more painting to do.

There was many a one that left these old red boxes, that got along well in the outside world with their knowledge of the three R's, especially 'rithmetic. Those that were way up in geography and grammar did not get along so well, on the average, for the time spent in those lines was taken off the more important three R's. These are the mainstay in getting along in the world. There are exceptions, of course: those that become schoolteachers, or that follow some special line that have to study what the custom calls for. Poor people do not have time to study everything, and if they did, everything is soon forgotten after leaving school, except what is used in everyday life.

Astronomy, geology, a lot of other "ologies," and a lot of languages are all right for those to know that like them and can afford them, but with rare exception they are about as useful to the ordinary mortal as two tails on a dog. It is not well to know just a little about everything and not much about anything. That class never got along except by a rare streak of luck. Along back, many parents sent their boys to college, even if they had to do without some actual necessities to do so. More recently, these boys have been coming out of college and could not get a job for as much as twelve dollars a week on the average. There are too many knowing the same things, and too little about any one of them. It is the specialist that "gets there," if he picks out the right line, and gets proficient enough to show his heels to the common rubble. He must have a gift for his calling and must keep clear of any calling that might become obsolete by some change.

In making a start, the "get rich quick" plan is no good. It is not safe. If your savings are put in a staunch savings bank, there is nothing any better, and if you hurry up and get a thousand or two dollars laid away and keep it there, you will have your own life insurance—instead of paying out premiums, you will have interest coming in, and the sum of these two will be your gain. Life insurance is a good thing in many cases, but there are a few young people that can duck it if they are smart. Lose your so-called friends, both male and female, that you have been wasting your money with. Let them call you a crank, a queer fellow, and other names. Keep your eye peeled for sharpers, and you will come out all right, and if you must do some business, be sure and employ a reputable lawyer. It is cheaper in the end. "A man that has himself for a lawyer, has a fool for a client."

If it is in your system, and you must speculate or bust, try a get-rich-slow play that is sure as anything can be. There are many. Here is one that has been tried out: Get four or five acres of cheap but rich rocky land, black soil preferred, and set it out to young, black walnut trees. They should be trimmed of all limbs except a few at the top. Set them thirty to forty feet centers, and take care of them once or twice a year, until they get big enough to be out of danger from cattle, and then let cattle graze amongst them. So far, there has been no worm that eats black walnut wood that I ever heard of. In twenty years, a tract of these trees will put any man on Easy Street. They might better have taught you this in school than some of the useless things you learned and forgot. Don't try buying real estate, expecting a profit from a raise in valuation. It does occur sometimes, and they find a gold nugget once in a while, also. They don't say much about the thousands that waste their time trying to find one. Your worry, your incidental expenses, loss of time, payment of taxes, loss of compound interest on the investment, will make a cheap piece of property a dear one in a few years, and in most cases, the savings bank would beat a real estate investment about a mile.

RELIGION AND WAR

There wasn't any [religion] to speak of, though there are plenty of churches, and though the people thereabouts are as good a class as I have found in any of the states, they do not fill the first require-ment. The first foundation stone of religion is to treat all mankind right, and that stone has never been laid yet. There is many a man no doubt that would come somewhere near it, if he had a chance. But, as he gets done in every side, he has to do likewise to others to get along—more's the pity! It is hard to fight a man with a club and win, unless you get a club yourself to have an equal chance. It has been said that the people are getting weaker and wiser. Be that as it may, they are certainly getting wickeder. Murder, kid-napping, rackets, stealing, and worse than all—war! About all they think about is making some infernal machines, poison chemicals, and the like to kill each other off in a horrible manner. If man was on the threshold of civilization at one time, as my friend said, he certainly isn't now. If we emanated from the monkey, and gained more wisdom than the monkey, then wisdom means murder. For the monkeys get along without wars, and live more sociable together than the so-called human race does. They don't use liquid fire nor poison gas to kill off a million or so of their own kind, and leave a lot dying by inches for years and years afterwards, as some of our soldiers have been doing, and are doing yet since the World War. The earth is not crowded yet. There is good land enough to supply all needs several times over. If a nation needs more land, why can't they buy it? It would be cheaper than to war for it. Or, if in need of a certain line of goods, why not make a contract with a country that would supply it cheap in large quantities?

The nations will have to get together and subdue any blood-thirsty brutes that like to strut in uniform before they get very powerful, if world peace is ever to be attained, and by the looks of things at present, they have waited longer than they should. A small war is better than a big one. If one nation controlled the whole world, it wouldn't be for long. They would split up, and have it all over again. The first rowdy nation that wants to start a fight, hit him on the head and chuck him out before he gets a following and a large supply of fighting tools. There are a lot of dumb Doras that think it cunning to raise a lot of boys for cannon fodder. Do they think if their nation should reign supreme over all other nations, that they would be fed on the fat of the land, and not have to work? The working class would be used worse than they are now. It is no wonder that Puck said, "What fools these mortals be!"

"War is hell," General Grant said, and it is hell for those left behind in many cases, as well as for those at the front.* On these rocky farms there were a lot of widows after the Civil War that were left with a few kids, and they sure had a tough time. Even up to the eighties, some were so hard put that they had their small crop of buckwheat ground hulls and all to make it go as far as it would. The hull of the buckwheat is quite poisonous, and it made even the grown-up children sick, as we found out afterwards, but they had to get used to it, or go hungry a part of the time. One bunch had about the poorest little bundle of rock of a farm there was in the country, or they would have got along better. The most intelligent ones had left home, and that did not help any. With some older hunters, I was with a bunch that passed their place, that was 'way back in from the main road, and the widow begged us to help her kill her pigs (that she had fed mostly weeds and apples) for her winter's meat. We felt sorry for her, so decided to forget hunting,

---

*Editor's note: This remark is generally attributed to General Sherman.

and dress her pigs. Some built a fire to heat rocks, some fetched water, found a barrel to scald them in, and at it we went. When we were through, we were tired and very hungry. She had cooled off parts of the first pig we dressed, and had a big potful cooked for us, and a stack of pancakes that was made of buckwheat that was ground hulls and all. They were as black as your hat. We paid no attention to that at the time—but we did pay attention several times before we got home. War sure is hell!

These widows drew ninety dollars a year after they got it, for many years, so they had a chance to live on the woodchuck fat of the land.

X

FROLICS

FROLICS (BEES)

The old timers of my father's time and before were rugged and tough as bears. They had to be to exist, but they had a heart, and up to about the middle eighties, if one got down, the others would help him up. But as time went on, the next generation got hardened, and seemed to think they had trouble enough of their own, without bothering with other people's, and if one got down they would kick him out in the gutter to get him out of the way, or what amounted to the same thing. Of course, they were not all that way, but if there was any help extended, it would not be from a universal source as formerly. When all the neighbors would pitch in, and do something, that was something.

As an example, a farmer got kicked by a horse, and his knee cap smashed, just as he was starting to put in his crops. It laid him up all summer, and left him with a straight leg for life. He had a bumper crop of grain and garden truck that year, and his stock was taken care of. First one and then another, when they could slip away from their own work, did the lighter part, and by having four frolics (called bees in the western states)—to put in his crops, get in his hay, harvest his grain, and draw up his winter's firewood—he was in a position to get through the winter, and his small children were provided for, and he resumed farming, gimpy legged, in the spring.

These frolics were the means of doing some jobs that were too big an undertaking for the farmer and his family alone, or perhaps to accomplish some undertaking to better advantage. Sometimes it might be a "raising." That consisted of erecting the frame of some building from timbers that had been "got out" in the woods, meaning that they had been scored, hewed, and mortised and tenoned. If the timber was dragged out first, there would be a lot of grit that would get in the bark, and it would dull the tools all the time. Even the chips were in better shape to finish into firewood if they went into the woods to get them, which they generally did and cut the tops in sled length for the same purpose.

When you went to town and passed a heap of timber near the site of a building, a bunch of men moving around it, and some women moving past the windows, and maybe an odd one outdoors after wood or water (they had come to help get the evening meal), then when you came back from town, even though you were gone only a few hours, there would stand the frame of a building, be it barn, dwelling, house, or granary. The carpenters that framed these timbers knew their "biz." Everything fitted like the paper on a wall. They were masters of everything from the twelve-pound broad axe to the little O.G. planes* that they made the entire window sash with, and had to shape their own planing cutters. All forms of molding were made in the same way for many years before the rotary power planing and molding mills came out, and window blinds were done by hand also; in fact everything was except sawing the boards, and not so many years previous so was some of that, one man down below the log, the other on top, pulling a saw up

---

*Editor's note: An ogee is a form used in molding that consists of two arcs that go in opposite directions. Thanks to Joshua Clark for noting that "it was one of the profiles used on the inside faces of the sash bars, rails and stiles of divided light sash windows." And that "some folks must have heard the name and assumed it was the letters O and G."

and down, following a chalk line. The "pitman," as the one below was called, had a cloth fastened over his head to keep the sawdust from going down the back of his neck, and a thin screen cloth over his eyes.

And, oh boy—what a kit of tools the old-time carpenters had. There was "chist after chist." The lot was plenty for a one-horse carload. Some of the tool chests themselves were made out of one-inch pine and were quite heavy, for they were large. Sometimes, in loading them, if the tools were in them, they were slid up on two skids, but generally they took the tools out, and after loading the empty box they were put in piecemeal. These chests were made with a construction inside that kept everything in its place, and from dulling. No simple construction. Nowadays, a carpenter can take his kit on his back, and even get on a trolley with it, and go to his job.

There were frolics to build "stun wall" fences, draw logs to the mill, build a dirt cellar, thresh grain, husk corn, and a number of other things. There were miles of stone wall built, and quite a large portion of it was built that way. Some of them now have been partly torn down, and the stones used to build the foundations of bungalows for the city people to come out and live in, in the summertime, and be alone. They come out for a rest and have to go back to the city to get it.

The logs were drawn to one of those old "up and down" sawmills, when they had a log frolic. The saw made a cut three-eighths of an inch wide, wasting a lot of lumber, but that kind of mill was all they had. The mill owner had a lot of sawdust to sell for insulating ice houses, so he got some good out of it. "Take your log to the saw dust mill" was a saying. After the steam-driven circular saws came out, and the way that they walked through a log, after seeing one of them and then looking at one of the old-timers, it gave you the impression that the saw went up one day and down the next.

The "flutter" water wheel that drove the old up-and-down mill had power enough to run the saw frame up and down faster, but if you turned on much water, the old mill would shake so, you would think it was going to walk away.

The building of a dirt cellar was quite a stunt. A hole was dug in a side hill piecemeal in advance of the frolic, when the "stun work" would be done. The side, back and front walls were laid first, with a doorway in the front wall with a lintel stone over it, all stones being picked out for their respective places, and having a flat outside face besides being shaped so as to stay put in the wall, and mind you, no mortar of any kind was ever used. The stones were laid so they couldn't shift their position, and then the voids "chinked" with smaller stones. The wall stones were shifted with crowbars, using "scotches" and "baits" with them as the conditions required.* There are a number of these walls in good shape to this day, as well as the balance of the stonework of the cellar type. After the walls were completed, then came the top. First there was a flat stone with fairly straight sides drawn by oxen and placed with about one-quarter of its length projecting over the cellar opening—one of these on each side, the two about matching each other for width; sometimes three pairs of these would reach from front to rear, and lap over the rear wall two or three feet. These stones were about twelve feet long, and projected over the cellar side walls three feet, and as the cellars were ten feet wide, they left a four-foot opening between their ends. Now comes the capstone, and this is considered big business! They rarely ever used two, unless the cellar was more than twelve feet deep. This flat stone had to be not less than fourteen feet square, but fourteen by sixteen would be used if one could be located not too far away. When one was found, it was slewed around with the "caut hook" and oxen, and if necessary, the edges trimmed with the "stun-hammer," and then the big rock chain was put around it, and three or four pair of cattle (as they called oxen) hooked on, the pairs being yoked in tandem. Geelong! and they all commenced to strain. Sometimes the chain would break and have to be mended with an old plow clevis and lots of wire, or with a shackle if the eye of the shackle would go through the link. That was seldom the case, for a standard rock chain consists

*Author's note: A "scotch" is a wedge placed under a rolling object to prevent it from moving or slipping. The use of "baits" here is unclear.

of the shortest links that can be forged, and the iron is very heavy in proportion. And then sometimes the chain would slip off, and maybe a nitch had to be made for the chain to go into the edge of the stone. Maybe the cattle couldn't draw it. If so, the log rollers in front of the stone that the stone would have gone up on if things had gone as well as hoped for, were put under the front end of the stone by the use of long pole levers, or maybe in the beginning someone yells, "She moves!" Once they got it on rollers, by putting those that roll loose in the rear around to the front they drew it along a little at a time. The most trouble was to find a route where the fast stones didn't chock the roller now and then. These routes were looked over in advance, and sometimes rocks had to be blasted. All the large flat stones were drawn up over timbers so placed that none of the previous stonework would be shifted, and exactly over where they were going to rest. Then, by use of long levers and scotching, they were carefully let down in place.

If their oxen had not been broken to do some things as accurate as humans, this work could not have been accomplished without going through a long and tedious routine. It's all right now to pooh-pooh what the old-timers did when looking at their work, but the first things that come to mind now are a derrick, a winch, a gasoline engine, and a tractor, none of which they had. "Golong" meant to them, go right along at regular speed, but "g-o-l-o-n-g" meant to just barely move what they were drawing, and they were also broken to stop at the word "woah" as though they were shot. In this way a stone could be stopped within a quarter of an inch, even if it weighed several tons.

After the stonework was all completed, there was four feet of dirt put over the whole business, and sodded over with transplanted sod, making sure that the four-foot dirt covering extended way beyond the outside edges of the large flat stones, for any stone of which the outer end gets bare in wintertime will have a white frost appear on it in the cellar. It is generally spoken of as the frost getting in the cellar. It is the heat getting out, and that makes the frost. The heat gets out so fast that the temperature falls below the freezing point on the inside face of the stone, and the cellar moisture freezes on it. Stone must be a fairly good conductor of heat for it to pass through eight or nine feet so readily. No wonder a stone-walled house will freeze you to death in winter, and roast you in summer, unless there is another wooden house built inside of it, or it is thoroughly insulated.

THE BUCKWHEAT FROLIC

Sometimes there is a buckwheat field away over in the back lots, remote from the barn, and there happens to be an old coal pit bottom that is sodded over, and is near to the field. There was generally a frolic to "thrash" the buckwheat there. To decide when to have it, they went by signs—the way the crow flies, the way the chickens act, and a lot of other things—one being that if the spider's webs were lying flat on the grass in the morning, instead of being tipped up at a slant, it was going to be a clear day. I never knew them to pick a stormy one. If they had, it would have made a mess of things. There was very much more clear weather, say fifty or sixty years ago, then there has been for thirty or forty years back, and there were very few of those grumbling or threatening days when you don't know what it is going to do—if you start in to do anything, or go anywheres, it will storm, and if you give up, it will clear off.

October was a banner month, and the forepart was when buckwheat was thrashed. There were generally two teams of oxen, though sometimes horses were used hitched to woodshod sleds, which were used on bare ground more than they were on snow during the year. The "shelvings" were put on the sleds and boards fastened on them, with canvas, old carpet, or some kind of rough cloth to catch as much loose buckwheat as possible. Then the tools were put on, two wooden scoops, six pitch forks, a fanning mill, a lot of "flails," two half-bushel measures, a "strike," and some extra pieces of bagging or old cloth, not forgetting a dried eel skin and an extra "boot ear" or two, as repair parts. The boot ears were put on the end of the flail staff to make a projecting loop that stuck out beyond the staff, and the eel skin was used to go through the eye of the swingle, and through the staff loop a few times and the ends fastened together to stay put, and leaving about two inches of clearance between the swingle and the loop. This boot ear loop was fastened on the staff by wrapping it with a homemade waxed end and the ends of the eel skin after being tied, and the shoe thread that the waxed end was made of is the same today as it was sixty years ago. They do not improve on anything, though they make many things worse.

It's time we started to the site of the operations. On arriving, the fanning mill and the rest are unloaded. The two teams start with two or three pitchforks, which may not be used at all, as the gavels are mostly picked up by hand and set on the sled in the same position they sat in the field, with the tip or grain end up. The coal pit bottom is being swept clean with a brush broom that was made right there in a few minutes, and it will sweep everything clean right to the roots of the short grass which a house broom would not be of any use for at all. Here comes a team with a load of gavels, and they are soon setting them on the pit bottom. This load will only cover half of it, leaving a walking-around space on the outside edge. Well, now the other load is set, and the flails begin to fly. Some are clearing away a place for the straw to be gotten out of the way, and let it rot where it is put, for it is no good for stock bedding, and it is bad to put on land, at least in that section. The flails are constructed with a staff made of straight-grained white ash, a little less in size than a broom handle, and about five feet long. The swingle is made from the best second-growth shatter bark hickory. It is about two and a half feet long, and one and three-quarters inches in diameter, with a scant three-quarter-inch eye in one end, and it soon gets a polish that makes it look like old ivory, and will almost sink in water. The handling of these flails has to be learned by a lot of experience. With a beginner, the swingle has a tendency to fly all over the place. Sometimes it will hit his elbow, and occasionally some have knocked themselves unconscious with one. After you have learned to make the swingle strike its whole length instead of on the point, and to keep the strokes uniform, you are almost there, but now you must learn to step around at the same time, and to land the blows where it will get the grain out evenly all over the "florin," as the coating of the straw and grain on the floor is called. (Although this is the same name given to the flax swingle, they are not alike at all. There is a threshing swingle and a flax swingle.) After you have learned to thresh alone, then you have to learn to "get in" with one, or maybe two or more. Four threshing together is considered too dangerous. No matter how many are threshing, an exact rhythm must be kept up, all the flails must strike at equal time intervals apart, and be lifted that way. With experts the end of the swingle when it is away up in the air generally makes a true circle in the air before it is brought down. It is an interesting sight, for those who have never seen three experts threshing.

After the gavels have all been threshed down flat, they generally go over the flooring once more, then they take a swig out of the old cider jug, and take a blow, while the "straw men" turn the flooring over, and it is threshed over again. Then the straw is picked up in small forkfuls and given a shaking to make any loose grain fall out of it, and pitched out of the way to be moved farther after, before the pile gets too big, and in the way of finishing the job. The teams are probably back by this time, the flooring of gavels is set again, and soon, until there is no more than enough threshed out than can be cleaned up before evening. There may be four or five inches of grain and chaff. The flooring having been raked off after each threshing, the fine chaff will not be more than twenty percent of the bulk, and the diameter of the flooring being only about twenty-five feet, the whole thing can be cleaned up in two hours or less. The fanning mill is set in a favorable place, with the tail end from the wind, so the chaff won't bother the workmen. A piece of cloth is laid down on the ground under the grain spout at the side of the mill. One half-bushel measure is set under the spout. The man that can turn the steadiest, neither too slow nor too fast, is put on the crank. A glance is taken in the tail end of the mill to see if the right screens are in for the buckwheat, and the connecting rod has been set to make the shaking frame travel the right distance. The crank begins to turn, and when the speed is fast enough, the feeder man begins to feed the mill with buckwheat, never too much in a chunk. By the time he starts, the other men have pushed up a large heap of grain with wooden pushers, and they keep a heap right behind him all the time, and keep the space gone over swept clean. As fast as one half-bushel measure is full, it is struck off, just level full, the empty measure being slipped under the spout quickly when the full one is taken away. The measure being taken away before it is struck will let a little grain down on the cloth, and also what is trucked off, but there will be plenty of time to dump the full one in a bag with the help of someone who stays with him to hold them open, and then scoop up the loose grain that was struck off, and the rest, and put it in one of the measures. The whole thing works like clockwork, and the loose straw is moved way over yonder before long. Then the last of the grain is swept up and put through the mill. The grain being measured and in bags, they and the old fanning mill and tools will be loaded on the sleds, not forgetting the big cider jug, which will probably be empty by that time. The procession will start for the granary, and unload the grain, and the fanning mill, if it belongs there, or it may be left on the sled that will take it home. After the men have gone in the house and had a big feed, the buckwheat frolic is over. Some of the neighboring women who came to help in the house will jump on a sled and ride home, if they are not watched, even if it is bare ground.

This way of doing it is a much better way than drawing it to the barn a little at a time, and threshing it on the barn floor.

CORN-HUSKING FROLIC

Frolics for building stone chimneys and fireplaces, using a certain kind of yellow clay found in the woods, were sometimes pulled off, but of minor import, for about three men can do it, or even two, to fairly good advantage.

And husking corn is the same. Frolics are rarely held for that purpose, unless a man gets behind in his work and they want to give him a chance to catch up. Then they do have one. And if it doesn't discommode the people in the house, they generally have a shindig that night. Because the work is very light, a boy ten years old can husk corn about as fast as a man, if it is a kind such that the ears will break off the stalk pretty easy. When one is held, the lumber wagon has the box body put on the boulsters, if it is not already on, and the wagon, or maybe two or three, are drawn to the cornfield, and left standing. The teams are unhooked, and let over some place and tied up to keep them out of mischief. Every family brings a two-eared corn basket so there will be at least one basket for each pair of huskers. The "stouts" are pulled over by catching hold of the band, and the part of the band where the ends are twisted together, or it may pull apart. The stout is not only pulled over, but is dragged just a little way, so as to pull up the center hill of corn that was not cut when the corn roundabout was, but left as a support to help hold the stout from blowing over, there always being so many rows cut each way to make the stout the standard size, though if the corn is extra heavy, the number of hills for each stout is lessened. The first thing after the stout is pulled over is to get out the jackknife and cut the stalks above the pulled-up roots of the center hill, to keep the dirt from bothering when biding the stalks, and from getting grit mixed with them. Then the band is cut, and one husker on each side of the stout gets down on his knees and partly sits on his heels. Spear by spear is drawn sideways, and the ears husked, and broken from it, and thrown at the corn basket that has been placed by the clear space where the stout had stood, taking care not to miss any ears or "nubbins," as the small and deformed ears are called. Then when the stout is finished, each half of the stalks is bound into a sheaf, by twisting a band of long, tough grass that finds time to grow up after the last killing of the corn. Sometimes there is not enough of this grass, and a few sheaves of rye straw are taken to the field for this purpose. These sheaves of stalks are left lying for the time being. Later, after a lot has accumulated on the field, they will be stood up, butts down, a certain number in a place, bound with a long band that can be handled better by two men than one. The butts are flared out at the bottom like the poles of a tepee, to brace it against the wind, and this outfit is called a "shock" of corn stalks. All forms of grain are put in shocks of this form before threshing takes place, buckwheat being an exception. It is a short-stalked grain, and is bound by grasping a handful of straw near the top, and by bringing the butt ends of the same straws up approximately. By passing it around the top, and sticking the butts in straight at the center, it makes binding enough, and the thing is called a "gaule."

Back to the corn. The corn basket is about full of corn, or will be after picking up what missed it, that was thrown at it during husking. This is carried and dumped in the lumber box wagon. Each pair of huskers is doing the same. Nearly every stout that is yanked over, the mice will run in every direction, and that is fun for the little terrier dog. And now and then a rabbit bobs out, and then there will be a great yip, yip, yippin'. The dog might better save his energy, for the rabbits will always beat him to a stone wall, or a woodchuck hole. Sometimes the rabbit will run under another stout and go on through, and out the other side, and before the dog finds out what is going on, the rabbit will be fifty yards away, only hitting the high places. If there are any women huskers, they will have a giggling spell.

When the wagon body is full, they will start in taking the corn to the other one, and the full one is then hitched on, and drawn to the granary, or corncrib, as the case may be. A corncrib is a rectangular box made of strong slats, except for the top and bottom, which flares out from the floor to roof, so rain blowing against it will drip down without touching the corn. The slats are left a little way apart, for ventilation, for if undried corn is stored in a tight place, it will get musty and moldy and rot. This crib is set up on posts, with the center of a tin pan on each post, the pan being turned upside down to prevent mice and rats from getting into the crib.

The corn doesn't grind so well that has been kept in a crib if there has been such wet weather. The best place for corn is in the top of a good tight-roofed granary, with plenty of windows for ventilation when the corn is first brought in from the fields, and the granary garret rafter is right there to hang the seed corn on, everything being shut up tight during wet weather. The corn is rarely brought to the barn to be husked, unless it is some that has been neglected until snow and ice have put in an appearance. The stalks are a nuisance in the barnyard. In the spring they have to be raked up, and taken away from the barn to burn them. Corn stalks are stacked out in the fields, and foddered out to the cattle mornings and sometimes evenings too. If there is a blizzard, or storm, that makes this bad business. The cattle are kept on hay at the barn altogether, at least the fodder portion; they have to be partially kept on it, anyhow, for the corn leaves do not have much food value in them. However, sowed corn, especially sweet corn, has as much food value as hay, because it is cut when the sugar is in the stalk, before it is converted into starch. And the stalks being small, the cattle eat the whole business.

And now that we have got the husking done, the stalks stacked, and the corn in the granary (pronounced grainery), as soon as it gets dry enough to grind good, we will take some to the mill, and then we will have "puddin'" and milk, and "Johnny cake"—maybe an Indian puddin' too.

XI

THE COUNTRY FAIR

There were California cucumbers that were as long as the ball bats, and twice as big. A pumpkin that weighed four hundred pounds. Two colors of tomatoes, yellow and red, through all the sizes from the current, the cherry, and the plum tomato on up to some that would not go into a two-quart dry measure, and weighed nine pounds. Rutabagas as big as nail kegs, cow horn turnips three feet long, cabbage heads sixteen inches across, a thirteen-inch ear of corn, etc. Most everything was big, even to the noise the band was making. The domestic animal exhibit was good and ranged from the little Shetland pony in the horse line through the different breeds to the enormous draught horses. And the bulls, oxen, steers, and cows came in for their share of admiration—hogs, fowls and sheep and what not. There was one sheep from some foreign country that had wool over a foot long and weighed around two hundred and fifty pounds. They had a hot-air balloon ascent. The fellow that went up performed on a trapeze underneath as it was yanking him rapidly up in the air. It must have been much harder for him to perform under those conditions. He "skinned the cat," hung by his feet on the bar, and went through all the other movements the same as though he had been in a gymnasium. That man had as much daredevil about him as anyone I ever saw, not excepting "Blondin," who walked from the United States into Canada on a wire stretched across the gorge just below Niagara Falls. After the balloon got about half a mile high and had drifted off to one side about an eighth of a mile, the top took fire, and the smoke and heat were let out so fast that it began to descend and with increasing speed until it landed in the tops of the tall trees of a dense swamp forest. The spring of the limbs cushioned things up, so he got off with a sprained ankle. When he was coming down, some of the women fainted, and the menfolk's hair was sticking up.

A tame bear bit a boy in the knee, and the owner of the bear was down on his knees sucking the wounds with his mouth, and half scared to death for fear that the boy's father was going to pound him.

A lady got shot with a Flobert rifle, but the bullet hit a corset steel and no serious damage was done.

They had a sign up front in a tent: "A horse with his head where his tail ought to be. Admission ten cents." Everybody who went in came out with a smile on their face, and when they were asked what it was, all they would do was grin, and finally those that had been asking all the time couldn't stand it any longer, and they went in, and then when they were asked, they had that same old grin. All it was: they had a horse tied with his tail to the manger, and his head to the back end of the stall.

A "barker" was yelling at another tent: "Right this way ladies and gents, only ten cents to see the wild man from Borneo, with hair on most everything, 'cept his teeth." (Probably captured right nearby.)

Another one had "One of the biggest ants the world has ever known. They have been known to pull up quite large trees, etc." This was another tent they came out of smiling, and that was all. It was really a big ant, all right—an eleph-ant.

They had some real good trotting races. One time there was an old black hoss, so poor that you could hang your hat on his hips, and count his ribs a hundred yards away. The races were decided by the best two out of three "heats." When this old black hoss came out to race, everybody laughed, and in the first heat he hadn't made much more than half the course when the rest had finished. The people saw then that he had only been put in the race just to make a laugh. At least they thought they saw. When the pistol was fired for the second heat, the black hoss suddenly disappeared from the bunch, and when they got about one-quarter around the track, the other hosses seemed to be wondering what became of him. In the next heat he did the same thing again. The farmers that had bet quite heavy on their favorites said "Ah-huh!" and probably some of them swallowed their cuds. And there were some other farmers who laughed so long, they fell off the old board fence that enclosed the track. How that rack of bones could get over the ground the way he did was one of the mysteries of the nineteenth century.

The womenfolks always had the big eats along, baskets full of roast chicken, "carliney pertaters," a big roll of butter fit for the angels, a big fruit cake, sometimes pound cake, lemonade, cold tea and common stuff galore, and a baked rice pudding. Oh, my gosh! It was made of rice that came from "Caroliny" also, it looked like glass, even after it was thoroughly cooked in the pudding, and the flavor of that rice pudding cannot be described on paper. Those large-sized, unbroken, crystal clear grains of rice that had a distinctive flavor of their own seem to be another good thing that is gone.

A bunch of friends, some from long distances and only seen once a year, used to get on the grass on the outskirts of the fairground, and spread one or more tablecloths down, and all sat around. And if there is anywhere on this earth a pleasanter place to be than at one of those friendly picnics at the country fair, I have never found it. Of course, there has always got to be a sad feature to everything—there were several faces missing from the year before, and a wondering of how many more would be missing next year. But apparently, all present decided that if their faces were to be "out of the picture" next year, they were going to get all the pleasure they could out of this one.

Many of the fairs have been done away with, and those that remain are not the same. And another grand old institution that used to tickle all the boys from seven to seventy is practically dead.

XII

Social Life

CHURCH SOCIALS

The church sociable was quite an affair with all the nice eats and soft drinks. But the old fiddle had to be quiet. They thought that anyone who danced would go to the hot place, for sure. They wouldn't even allow church music played on a fiddle, for they said, "The devil is in a fiddle, anyhow." I tried to tell them if that was the case, the only way to get him out was to play it, but it wouldn't work. Those that had charge of things knew that most of the people present danced sometimes, and it just would not do. No, not even after the preacher went home. Some of them had so much dance pent up in their system that they "throwed themselves" when they went to the next one. There is always a fly in the ointment. Some of them were unsociable enough to get off in a corner and talk about some of the others.

A week or two before a wedding was coming off, the skimmerton boys were busy getting their noise-making outfit in working order. And the women were making everything in the kitchen fly, from the jiggering iron (that makes a roll or butter look like a pineapple) to the large-sized dripping pans. For, believe me, they had the grand eats at those weddings. In the meat line, there were turkeys and all other barnyard fowls, and if the wedding was in the wintertime, as most of them were, they had what was considered the best meat of all—spareribs!—that had been hung up in a cold garret to age a month or so, and acquire a flavor all their own. No salt was ever put on them except what little was needed when they cooked. And then the cakes! What a variety—from jumbles to pork cake, that would keep moist and improve in flavor for a lifetime, if it could be hid where it would not be discovered. There was marble cake, jelly cake, gold cake, silver cake, fruit cake, and cake that would start to melt before you could get it in your mouth, and after you got a piece of that you never bothered to find out what the other kinds were. And sweet meats (as all kinds of preserves were called), apple quinces, old-fashioned red plums that had to have a pound and a quarter of sugar to one pound of plums, with the pits in, which was the secret of their grand flavor, and then the native citron, red currant jelly, quince jelly, and rummet cider red as a cherry, and so thick it would stick to a glass, and blackberry wine that would make you feel like you could go right across country and only hit the high places.

After the fowl course was finished, the table was quickly cleared and reset with cakes without those at the table leaving their seats. And honestly, when some of those settings were completed, the table looked as much like a flower display as it did a bunch of eats, the effect being produced mostly by skillful use of the jiggering iron, the various bottles of colored sugar, and some paper flower stencils that gave the outlines.

A jiggering iron was a contraption that had a wheel at one end that when rolled along made a track that looked like where a hen had crossed the road, but on a smaller scale, of course, and on the frostings of cakes, the balance of the vine being completed with the other end, which had a half moon, and the cage being "pinked" or zigzagged. When this was pressed down, it made the outline of half the edge of a leaf, and by turning it halfway round, and pressing down with the two points touching, you had the other half. On pies, the vines, etc. were left plain. But on cakes, the leaves were filled in with green sugar, the vine with sugar of about chocolate color, the rose and other red flowers with red, of course, and the center of the rose filled with gold-colored sugar (a mixture of madder and sugar) or the mixture of sugar with the yolk of an egg.

The sugar bottles were plugged by corks with turkey quills through them, with a little cut off the end, so a very small stream of sugar could be directed where wanted. By wetting only the parts where the sugar should stick with a camel's hair brush and waiting for one color to dry before the next one was put on, a very neat-looking job could be done. Some said, "Them air cakes is jes to pertie to stick a knife in."

At one of these weddings the skimmerton boys had gathered around, everything was cooked, and the old long table was almost breaking down with turkeys and all other kinds of barnyard fowls, and two heaping eight-quart pans of spare ribs. There was some excitement in the dining room that drew everybody out of the kitchen. The skimmerton boys took advantage of that. They quickly lifted the window, one jumped in, and swiped what they all considered the best there was—a pan of spare ribs!

WEDDINGS

The riding of "skimmerton," as it is called here in the East ("shiveree" in the West), begins with the making of enough noise to jar the mood down, or whatever happens to be around, sometimes a few window lights. This is done as a self-introduction. If the door opens, and someone says hello—or what in hello!—the chairman of the committee will step forward and make known the demands of the boys, which if the parties are pretty well fixed, will run about like this: Bring the bride to the door, so that all may see her. Roll out a barrel of good cider, hand out one eight-quart pan of spare ribs, one six-quart pan of jumbles, and a large fruitcake. If their request is complied with, there will only be a reasonable amount of noise made by blowing horns and conch shells for two or three hours, when the boys will disperse and go home, those around sixty generally going first. If the door doesn't open, or their demands are ignored, it is just too bad for the parties involved. There will be a lot of damage done then, unless the parties come in time before it goes too far. As a fair warning before they start, they let off the old cannon (that was large enough to make it necessary to strap it to a pole so as to carry it on their shoulders), and maybe burst some old obsolete guns that were loaded to destruction, and the trigger pulled from a distance with a string and from behind a rock or building. (There was many an old flintlock gun that went that route, that would be worth money now as a relic.) They all had their coats turned wrong side out, and their faces marked with burnt cork or paint, so their own mothers would not have known them, so nothing could be proven by anyone peeking out the windows, or by those that might happen to pass by—in case there was damage done, and the parties tried to put the law on them.

At one time, (though the house is gone long ago) there was a preacher that lived near the top of a young mountain, with open sloping fields off down to a little bramble-covered valley about an eighth of a mile away. There had been a very deep snow, and a rain on top of it that froze as it came, until there was about two inches of ice that could be skated on anywhere, and this ice stayed on for more than a month. It was known as the icy winter, and at this time his daughter was getting married, and the skimmerton boys were on hand. They let off a few ordinary guns, but it was no use. Nobody opened the door. He thought because he was a preacher they would not damage anything, but he never made a bigger mistake in his life. He happened to be one of the preachers that did something else besides preaching, and was well fixed. After being totally ignored, the boys went to work.

The next morning, the pickets were all off the fence, and his little outbuildings had found a new site. His horse's harness was not in the barn, and to cap the climax his light wagon was astraddle of the peak of his barn, with the wheels and all on. The front and rear wheels were tied together to keep it from rolling forward or backward. There wasn't much danger of its blowing over sideways. How they got it there is still a mystery, and always will be, for all of those that helped put it there are gone, and the young boys that went to see it are nearly all gone, too. It took half a dozen men with a lot of tackle and a couple of long poles to lean against the barn for it to slide down on that they dragged from the woods to keep from breaking it.

Someone happened to see something sticking to a bush that stuck up a little above the ice, and on investigation with the use of ice spurs, it was found to be a bridle. That gave them the cue that probably the rest of the harness was somewhere off down the hill. It was all found—a piece here and a piece there, a long way from the barn, where they had lodged against a large rock or something—except the collar, and that was found the following summer by someone picking blackberries over an eighth of a mile from the barn. For many years after that, those that rode skimmerton got better treatment, for it was cheaper in the end.

Finally, there were so many people gone away that there was not enough to have a decent wedding party, and what was left was in much poorer circumstances. What few weddings pulled off was done by going to someone capable of "tying the knot," and then going off for a trip. There was sort of a sick attempt to have a little blowout when they returned, but they never amounted to much, and from then on the married couple never had the laugh on their scattered neighbors, until their neighbors had to do all the work, lugging them around to get them to the grave.

DANCE, MUSIC

These farmers and their children sure had their fun when the opportunity afforded. One way was when the snow was packed down and the roads were well broken. Out would come the old homemade woodshod sled, and on it would go the lumber wagon body. This was filled even full of clean rye straw, and after the oxen were yoked to the sled tongue, all hands piled in and away they went to some dance. The oxen were slow, but who cared? Everybody was having fun, and the bunch would make more noise than a spring pond hole full of quacker toads. If horses were used, in getting by the other teams they would have to go maybe into deep snow at the side of the road, and they would flounder around so they were liable to break the harness or get in some other scrape.

Owing to the continuous intensity and duration combined, it is doubtful that any part of mankind has ever experienced more pleasure in one chunk than they did at those old-time square dances, quadrilles, cotillions, shindigs, call them what you like. As soon as the old fiddle started and a bunch commenced to hoe it down, the crowd caught on to the rhythm of the thing, and went into a trance that they never came out of till morning—the lookers-on as well as those dancing, when maybe some old codger would come in from outside and bawl out, "Gosh all hemlock, if it ain't broad daylight!" "Oh, they dance all night, till broad day light, and went home with the gals in the mornin'." These dances are a thing of the past, and have been these many years. The winters got milder, and the roads full of mud, and hubs [?] instead of snow. There got to be such a scattered sprinkling of farmers, and as soon as their children grew up they would "fly the coop," so there was no one to save a dance of the old-time kind. There has been plenty of dancing done since in places set apart for the purpose, in small huddles. The lancers, the Saratoga Lancers, and many other dances on down to the Big Apple of the present day, have been put on the boards. But the people just don't get the same kick out of them somehow. Along in the eighties some of the farmers told some of the summer boarders about the fun they had at the winter dances, and the city people became interested to such an extent that they had to try it out somehow, so they got a country fiddler one night, and after clearing everything out of the dining room, they went to it, and although there was a lot of perspiration lost, it took! It made so much extra work, however, that they were told that if they wanted to do any more dancing, they would have to do it in the barn, saying it as a joke—but the city folk didn't take it as a joke. With the country folks laughing at them, they swept the loose straw and chaff off the barn floor, moved out the old fanning mill, the flails, and whatever else was in the way, lit the barn with kerosene and Japanese lanterns, and the barn dance was born!

There were a few old-time fiddlers who could make music that would penetrate into where you live. There are some people alive today who have heard almost everything from Gilmore's and Sousa's bands on down through orchestras, who would rather hear one of those old-time expert fiddlers than anything they have ever heard in the way of music. Noah Webster says in his dictionary that "the sweetest music is played by ear," and if it is produced by an expert, he is right. Musical sounds come first, and any improvement in them must come originally from the musician. A plan was conceived to put audible sounds onto paper in visible form, and then from this visible form, convert them back into the original sounds. This is the so-called note system. If the notes are written from hearing one of those old-time fiddlers, and someone who plays by note tries to reproduce it, it is as much of a misfit as a square pin in a round hole. It has been tried time and again without success. It is true the framework of the piece is there, but there must be a lot of refining sounds added to it, and bad ones taken from it, before it duplicates the original. It is just as hard to catch all the compound, complicated, and sweet blended sounds or harmony that a first-class fiddler can produce, that plays by ear, as it is to catch a bottle of sunshine and keep it for a rainy day. All music today is written to comply with the note system, a case of the tail wagging the dog. On some instruments it doesn't make much difference, but it does on a fiddle. These old-time fiddlers didn't have any super-grade fiddle, or violin, if you like to call them that. There is only twenty dollars difference between the two, anyhow. You pay twenty-five dollars for a new violin, and when you get hard up and want to sell it, it is a secondhand fiddle, and you get five dollars for it.

The lady who won the championship playing at the Chicago World's Fair paid twenty-five dollars for hers new, so why pay more? One old fiddler said he traded a cow for his, so I guess it wasn't a Stradivarius but maybe just as good, for that Stradivarius stuff is mostly fake. The genuine article is in all probability about as scarce as hens' teeth now, and the quality of what few there are is much overrated. Otherwise, they must have fallen in poor hands, or their owners would be winning all the prizes, or at least gain an extraordinary reputation. Of course, some may be kept as antiques.

One of the vehicles of pleasure that has passed away is the one known as a sleigh, sometimes called a cutter, with its offset shafts so the horse didn't have to travel on the comb of the road, and its seat well equipped with buffalo robes. The sound of a string of sleigh bells is no longer heard in the land, and some young fellow who took his best girl for a sleigh ride is beginning to be spoken of as a man of ancient history.

But in the place of the horse and sleigh, or the buggy, more recently something came along that gave a lot of pleasure to many people who could afford it, until the novelty wore off, and that was the old Model T Ford car. There were a number of people when they had their first ride in one of these cars that acted as though they thought they were in paradise. It was the first car that could be depended upon to "take you there and bring you back," and once in a blue moon, if you happened to run into a stone wall or something, a piece of old bale wire would fix it up, and you could come on back home.

No ride in any high-priced car has ever touched the spot like my first one in that old Model T, and if it had a middle speed, it would be hard to beat for many purposes right now. I wouldn't be a bit afraid to go coon hunting in it, and run it right up the tree and shake one out.

If the fellow on a small rocky farm can sport a small car, a radio, and a canning outfit, to can everything in sight to help him through the winter, he is not so bad off these times, considering the way they have changed in the outside world. But if he sells a fatted calf, he better do it on the sly, for if the assessor finds out, he will have his taxes raised.

VALENTINES

There used to be outlandish valentines with the most awful pictures, and verses of the most insulting language that the law would allow printed. And they were of great variety. There could always be one picked out that would hit anybody's "sore spot." Big nose, big feet, short folks, tall folks, busybodies, liars, cheats, and one to fit any kind of occupation, and when you received one of them, you got an awful picture of yourself, that would magnify to an enormous extent any little or big abnormal feature or eccentricity you possessed. And of all the lambastings you would get from the verses! The idea was to make a person hopping mad, without letting them know who sent it.

Those receiving one almost always guessed the wrong sender, but the fur would fly just the same. There were tongue lashings, slamming of doors in each other's faces, and almost hair pullings around the valentine season. It wasn't uncommon to see a couple of ladies pass each other with heads straight up, as though they had each swallowed a broom handle, and eyes straight to the front, with never a word. They had been best friends before the valentine came. This epidemic raged for several years. About a standard case was something like this:

One woman would go and knock on her neighbor's door, and when it opened she let go. "You had little to do to send me a valentine about my big nose! You needn't think you can fool me. You went to New York last week, and your letter had that post mark on it. 'Nother thing! I know that writing of yours, even though you tried to disguise it. There ain't no one else on earth that makes an aitch like you do. I'll have you to understand that my nose ain't as big as your feet!"

"Ahah! So it was you that sent me one about my big feet, eh? You dirty hussy! And now you are over here trying to make out I sent you one about your nose, to throw me off the track!" And then the main pieces of fireworks went off. They both screamed together, both talked together, like chained lightning, and neither one understood a word of what the other said. They kept it up until apparently the one inside got out of breath first, and SLAM went the door.

There was a nice young clerk in the store that everybody liked, and nobody ever dreamed that he had anything to do with valentines, except to sell them over the counter. But he was a joker. He was in a position to get familiar with handwritings as well as see and hear a little of this and that, that he could use to advantage, and by fixing it with a friend to have letters mailed at a distance, he could play cards very ingeniously.

Many years after, when he thought he was safe from getting his hair pulled out, and the old store was a thing of the past, he "let the cat out of the bag." He caused much more laughing than he did quarreling, so it was probably all for the best. It taught a lot of people that they should not be too quick to blame others on circumstantial evidence.

Appendix I

Country Dialect

I am not going to = I haint goan to

I told you so = I tote you so

Something = Sumthin or suthin

What is the matter, pop = Smatter pop

He threw a stone = He hove a stun

He is throwing stones = He is heaving stuns

Suppose he does = Spose he does

Yanking = Yankin

Potato = Pertater, and tater

It is none of your business = Snun o your bizness

It isn't yours = Taint yours

If I ever catch him = Fi ever ketch im

Tobacco = Tub-accur

He asked me = He assed me

I expect he did = I spect he did

Who is he = Whos zee

It isn't yours, it is mine = Taint yourn smine

More than would fill a kettle = Morned fill a kittle

It is nobody = Snow body

Radishes = Redishes

Pumpkin = Punkin

Cucumbers = Cowcumbers

It would not do = Twondent do

It is my fault = Smy folt

Pigeon = Pid-gin

Pudding stick = Puddin stick

I shall not tell you again = I shant tell ye agin

Just for fun = Jis fer fun

Go on = Gwaun

Did you go = Jew go

Did you ever see such = Jever see sich

Did you have any fun = Jew enny fun

Just as I was going to shoot, he jumped in his hole = Jist zi wus
goan t shute, he jumped in his hole

I am certain of it = Im sartin uv it

Won't you come = Woontche cum

Well of all things = Well fall things

Will you have a chew = Will ye hev a chaw

And I don't care = Ni doan care

Enough said = Nuff sed

He knows his business from A to Z = He nose his bis from a to
issard

What do you mean by saying that = Whatya meen be sayin that

He is a beef eater = Hees a bee-feeter

Will you have an apple = Will ye hev a napple

It was an egg =It wuz a neg

I am kind of unsteady = I'm kindy onstiddy

It is too bad = Its stew bad

It isnt' him, it is the other one = Taint him its tuther one

It is enough to make you sick = Snuff to make you sick

I will bet you = Ile betcha

He climbed a tree = He clum a tree

Onion = On-yin, ungin, ung-yin

Who are you = Hoo be yew

Just as likely as not = Jeslikeisnot

Asparagus = Sparrygrass

Tomorrow = Tmar, tomer

As if = Ezeff

And why = An why

Trouble = Trubill

It is an awful thing = Snawful thing

Toolchest = Tool chist

That is another lie = Snother lie

Somebody = Sumbuddy

I had ought to = I dortee

It is as much as I can do = Smutch zi kin dew

Thicker than hair = Thickern hair

He went courting = He went coutin

The devil's imps = The devil zimps

Partridge = Patridge

Horse = Hoss

Titman = The pig that has no tit of his own. Meaning undersized when born, this name applies to undersized people.

Middle-sized pigs = Shoats

Sit in the rocking chair = Set in the rockin cheer

Pears = Peers

I can do without = I kindew thout

It looks as though he done it = Looks zif e dunnit

He bored it with an auger = He bored it with a nawger

Cigar = Sig-gar

Mixed ale = Micks tail

It smelled = It smelt

It isn't his = Taint hissen

Women = Wimmin

Steady company = Stiddy company

It is more than I can do = It smore ni kin dew

Salt = Salt pronounced with a sound as in *ah*

Why did you pick so many = Wyd ye pick smenny

Yes = Yep

No = Nope

Well I will be gol darned = Lile be goldarned

The whole length = The hull length. The *u* in hull being in the same key as the *oo* in wool.

Being as it is you = Beansit yew

However = Howsomever

I do not remember = I disremember

Suppose he does not = Supposen he dont

Besides I do not know = Sides I dunno

Maybe this will hold you a while = Mebby this il hole ye a spell

Who is he to come in like that = Whozee tew cum in so

Have you ever seen one = Hev ye ever seed wun (This last is not
  common. In fact, there is quite some difference in the dialect
  within a radius of five miles. In some parts they say *saft* for *soft*,
  and there is some fun made of each other, when neither one is
  right. That makes outsiders laugh.)

Grist mill = Gris mill

Until the cows come home = Till the cows cum hum

Yellow dog = Yeller dorg

Who is that = Whos zat

The house is haunted = The house is hanted

So far and no farther = So fer an no fudder

It is the worst ever = Tis the wust ever

More than enough = Moren enuff

Faucet = Fasset

Are you mad at me = Be you mad to me

I dare not = I dassent

Wrestle = Rassel

I have got enough = I got enuff

Rabbit = Rubbit

The whole length = The houl length

I expected = I spected

Varment = Varmint

Experiment = Sperimint

Trousers = Trowzis

Suspenders = Galluses

Nervous = Narvus

Yessir = Yarser

Grease = Griss

I earned it = I airnt it

Hiccough = Kick-cups

By and bye = Bynby

Author's note: There is a long lingo in the commands of oxen, and it is strictly adhered to, so the oxen do not become confused by change of drivers. The ox learns slow but well, and it is surprising what a team and driver can do with them, if both know their stuff.

APPENDIX II

THE VISIT

Knock, knock, knock! She opens the door.

"Well, fer lands sakes! If it ain't Sumanthy! How be ye? Come in! Take off your things. My, what a purty alpackey shawl you got. I'm tryin' to save up enough to git one. The storekeeper told me they be goin' up. He said they come all the way from South Americky. What's been keepin' you away so long? What's all the news?"

"Well, to begin with, they come out and tried to git me in. In one place they said that had just took a panful of sourcream shortcake out of the oven, and had some fine bass wood honey, and citron preserves. But I told 'em I started out to see Hanner, and Hanner it was goin' to be. What a nice easy rockin' chair this is! I like the crook o' the back better'n mine. When you are tired, the rockin' chair is the oney thing."

"Wait til I git t'other one out of the front room, and put on some water to bile, an' set the old earthen teapot on the back of the stove to be warmin' up. It's tempered so it's as black as ink, an' wait till you see what sweet tea it makes. Be back in a minnit!. . . . Well, the water is on, now. First, let's hear what kept you away so long."

"Well, there has been just one thing after another. Lenny has an awful stuffed toe on his left foot, and a stun bruise on his right heel. He hain't fit to go to school nor do nothin'. He hobbles around some on the tow of one foot, and the heel of t'other one.

There is no use of talkin', he is bound to go barefoot. They's no use to buy shoes, he's got a pair of boots that would be plenty good enuf to wear in the summertime, even if the toes is cut. He wore 'em through stearin' his sled ridin' down hill belly gut last winter. If I live to a nother winter, I'm goin' to buy him a pair of them brass-toed boots, that has been out a spell. Some tried 'em out last winter, an' they was all right in the spring. An' Bobbie, he's bin quite sick for a few days back, and had a nawful cold, and some fever. I give him some mountin mint tea last night when he went to bed, and put a little white snakeroot in it, to break up the fever. He looked kind o' peeked this mornin'. He's never been just right since he had the hoopin' coff, but was a settin' around, and all along back things too numerous to mention turned up to bother me. You don't come to see me for months an' months, anyhow. I know you say your bunion hurts, if you walk fur. Seems to me your man ought to drop you over my way once in a while. When they stopped me at the fust place comin' along, one of 'em took me to one side, an' told me that that big haw buck of a feller that lives over on dug way is goin' to marry Em Sidler in a month or two. They don't want anyone to know it, but I found out by accident. Don't tell anyone, whatever you do! At each of the next two places, one of 'em took me to one side and tole me exactly the same thing. And I'm tellin' you, and don't give a pinch o' snuff who you tell so long's you don't tell who told you."

"It must have come from that one over the hill. How she knows about all things comin' to pass, long before they do, is beyond me. She must do it by instinked, or somethin'—Back in a minnit! The water must be bilin', take a few minnits now for the tea to draw—Less, see—where did you leave off?"

"Oh, I got through withthat, an' now I want to hear something from you."

"Well, things been runnin' along 'bout the same. Mebbe I better start in with a couple of city fellers that come up to fish, and went back a few days ago. They are the ones we have knowed so long. My man went down to see 'em last winter fer a few days, they had begged him so long to come. He told me when he was walkin' on the sidewalk down there, every once in a while he ketched someone grinning at him, if he looked off to one side quick. He had on his black suit an'all, and he couldn't see what they were grinnin' at. He got at his friends to know what was the matter with him. He said they tried to put him off, but he wouldn't have it. He told them they had been good friends, and they must tell him. They said, "Now, don't git mad, an we'll tell you'. . . . Tea must be drawed, be back in a minnit!"

"My! But that is good tea. I see you drink black tea, same as I do."

"Yes, I had to, the green tea gives me canker sores in my mouth an' I had to make a tea of scavish root to pucker em up, and drive 'em away. Didn't take me long to git used to the black, an' now—about them two fellers I was tellin' you about. They told him it was because he we liftin' his feet so high when he walked, an' that he had got the habot from steppin' over stones in rocky country, an' was a backwoods farmer. He said he tried to sluff his feet along after that, but he would git to lookin' at a high buildin' or somethin', an' up they would come again. When the fellers was there they said they liked our butter, chickens, eggs an' everythin' better than in the city. But I noticed they didn't eat any sallit. I asked them after a day or so, at the table, 'Why don't you eat some sallit? An' one of 'em said, "What's that?' I pinted at a large tater bowl full that was on the table. He took a little of it out on his plate, and tasted it, an' then ast if it was a rellish. I didn't know what a rellish was, no more than he did sallit, so I said, 'I don't know.' He laughed, and ast if it was growed around there. I said sure, out in the garden. After dinner he went out to see it. It was sowed same as we all sow it, so thick that when it grows up the sun can't shine on it, and the stalks grows five or six inches long as white as snow. At the top there is just a little green streak where the sun hits a part of the time, an' the rest of the leaf about the size of a silver dollar that the sun hit all the time, is brown, an' that is why they call it old fashion brown sallit. You know all about that, same as I do.

He tasted it, an' said it tasted like some kind of lettuce,* an' a very delicate kind, at that, an' ast me if I would put some after washing it, on the table just as it is, an' I said sure. I put a big platter full on at the next meal, an' they would take a spear at a time, put a little salt on it, and nip it like a dog eatin' grass. Semms like they thought they ought to eat some for medicine purpose, but affeared to eat mutch. All they took if it had been wadded up, wouldn't have made a ball bigger'n a hen's egg. But they said it was the best lettuce they ever eat. I had enough on the table for a dozen at that rate. I thought they was goin' to do somethin' with it. I showed him how we cut it close to the ground with an old pair o' scissor, an' left the roots where they were, so as to keep the grit and dirt off it, an' told him that we always raised our own seed. I told him I always washed and cut up a four quart pan full, if there was five or six to eat, an' then mixed cane syrup an' vinegar together until the tang was just right, and kept sprinklin' it in, an' stirrin' up until it was all hit. He laughed, an' said he bet he could learn to eat it that way. When they went away, they left my man a box of ceegars, an' they must have just been made, or somethin' for when he smokes one, he says when he gits about half way down, there's so much juice, he can't tell whether he is smokin' or chewin'. That's them on the chimbley shelf, dryin' out. I wish he wouldn't use tobaccur, but I snuff, so I hev to keep still. An' now, let's hear from you. Hev you bin over to see Abbie since she broke her leg?"

---

*Author's note: The word "lettuce" is a newcomer, comparatively. I never heard it until I was a big boy. All forms of that is now called lettuce was called *sall it*, or *sallit*. The first package of seed that came from a store with lettuce on it, we didn't know what it was by name, but the picture told us what it was, and some kicked about changing the names of things so. It may have been called lettuce in the dictionary at the time, but I doubt it. There was one in the school if I had thought to look, and now I am wondering if the word *sallit* was in it, and for that matter if it is in it now? We had raised our own sallit seed for maybe ten years straight when we got a new kind from the store to see what it was like, and that is where the word lettuce was born so far as we were concerned.

"Yes, I went over about a month ago. My man had to go over by there to see about buying a pair of cattle, and dropped me off until he come back. She was hobblin' around with crutches. She told me the boys along back tapped her a lot of sap trees, an' cut her enough wood to bile the sap. It froze one nite before morning, and when she went out to see if any of the things had sap enough on 'em to freeze an' bust. Naturally, the first thing she picked up was her teapot. Just as she picked it up, she slipped on some frozen sap that had been spilled, an' broke her leg. She said she didn't care so much about her leg, if she hadn't broke her teapot. She said it was tempered as black as the stove, and made tea as sweet as honey. It was really too bad, she ought to have knowed better than to put every thing she had out. But I suppose she hain't got many things to put out. She has been along there now for fifteen years, come next October. If the neighbors didn't send her a beef's pluck, and take her a quarter o'tea and three and a half pounds of sugar once in a while, I don't know how she would git along. Cy's boy was takin' her a quarter of tea in his coattail pocket, and got ketched in a shower, an' his coattail wet through, an' or course, that old yaller brown paper that is made from straw dissolved, that they always make them little printed packidgis with, for small stuff. It all went to smuck, and she had to do the best she could to get the tea separated from the lints that was in his pocket. She said it was a wonder they wouldn't make decent paper to do stuff up in. All that yaller brown stuff is good far, is for the boys to chaw up to make wads for their popguns. She talks so funny. She says 'peers' fer pares. 'I hearn 'em say so,' for 'I heered 'em say so.' She says 'cain't' fer can't, an' such like. I feel sorry for the poor old thing. It's easy to see she hain't got mutch edgicashin. 'Tain't her fault, though. There was so many of 'em, and so mutch work to do, that half of 'em went to school one day, an' the other half hoed corn, turn about, an' when they got to hayin' on it, they changed to stirrin' hay the same way. An' later on, diggin' taters in the fall, or huskin' corn, an' she told me all the books they had, ceptin' borried ones, was a new spellin' book, an' an old 'rithmetic, that was half dogs' ears, and a lot of leefs lost out. Anyhow, it don't bother her none, an' when you come to think of it, no grate larnin' is needed nowadays. If a body knows all about pounds, shilln's an' pence, an' can figuer a little, like you an' me, that's near enough, an' know a little about that new 'dismal' system. The only trouble is we don't git money enough to count to keep from fergittin' how. One says 'twenty-five cents,' an' t'other says 'two shillin'.' Do you suppose they thought the money would go further by countin' it two ways? Ten cents, one dime, ten dimes, one dollar. All foolishness! We could make any kind of change with farthings, ha'pennies, and cents. They done one thing, tho, that I like, bringing out them little pennies instid of them old big copper ones. An' them little things dyin' out, like the three cent silver shad scale, an' the six square gold twenty-five cent pieces. They would git lost when you are lookin' right at 'em. The four and tuppence, an' such is hardly ever heard of now. And then, we kin read an' spell goodnuf to git along, an' I kin always git some of the big girls to write what little I want, an' in a pinch I can write better'n Horace Greely myself."

"Well, I'm glad to hear she is getting' better, anyhow. Wait, till I run in the seller, an' get some bread, butter and preserved straw-berries, an' cake. Be back in a minnit. . . ."

"My, but them strawberries do taste good!"

"They be good, if I did do them up. T'other day me and Mandy put our ole sunbonnets on, an' went over to one of them back side hill pasture lots. The whole hillside was red. I got twelve quarts an' Mandy ten. Ain't it queer that some wild things is better'n tame ones. There was some wild vines got mixed up with the tame ones on the edge of the tame patch, an' got cultivated without our knowing it. When we went to pick some tame ones, we seen oversized wild ones, with deep seed holes, an' quite long little necks between the berry an' the hull. We thought we would have a few right there, an' we got fooled. They were just as sour as the tame ones. Everything to its own nature! We tried to have arbutus grow near the house. We thought that if we put it under a tree on the north side of the house, we might fetch it, but it didn't work. An' we done our best with wild lady slippers, but they pined away. And some of the darned things was growin' and blossomin' as nice as you please in jest a little green moss that was on a flat rock. Say, while I think of it, does your man ever go near that graveyard in the woods with the white marble tombstones? One of my grand-pops lays there."*

"Yes, he went up that way after squirrels and pidgins last fall, an' he said some of the trees were nigh as big as barrels, an' the root had got so big that they had moved the tombstones so they canted away over, an' he said there was moss on one side of 'em, an' none on t'other. The letters was mostly plain yet, if they hap-pened to be on the side with no moss on it. He said if only he knowed how to read, he could have told who was buried there. There is lots of them little graveyards that have no white stones at all, just flat stones stuck up with nothing on at all. For white stones they must be very old, though not as old as some red brown stones that is in some of the big graveyards, that was put up before the revolutionary war. The stun they was made from they say came acrost the ocean as ballast on a ship from some far away country. An' it is a great weatherin' stone, for a lot can be read on 'em yet. We will be into one a long time, an' the time will soon begin, so let's talk about somethin' else. Oberdier's boy walked to town tother day, an' it's all of eight miles, an' gawked around. When he came back, the naburs could hardly live with him for a few days, account of his telling them 'bout seein' a man that had a box all painted up that he stiddied with one leg, like a crutch that was a little too short. Said he had a strap from the box over his shoulder, an' when he stood up straight, the leg didn't touch. But when he stood it down, an' bent over, an' turned a little crank, what sweet music the thing made, an' he had a monkey with him, 'cause I seen one's picture in the geography, an he looked putty nigh like some men in the face, an' knowed just as much, for when they throwed down pennies, he grabbed 'em an' took 'em to his boss, an' that

---

*Author's note: There are no authentic graveyards in this section that hold Indians. I presume they were the kind that put the dead up in trees. Any time the oldest graveyards were investigated, there were iron nails found that had been hand forged of wrought iron.

is more than some men could do. They told him it was an organ grinder. Well, he went to town again in a few days, an' when he came back, he said he seen another feller, with something slung on his back, an' his monkey must have been sick, for he wasn't with him. He said he follered him around, block after block, until he was tired out, but all he would do is ring a bell, and wouldn't set it down, an' play a tune. My man told him, 'You darned fool, that was nothin' but a cissers' grinder!' Well, I muss be goin' for hum. It's gettin' late by yer new Seth Thomas clock. They be a fine clock, an' no weights for the children to grab. One thing about stayin' later than I dawt to, is, I will heve a good excuse for getting' by the houses goin' back.

"Well, if you must go, take these carnation pinks, an' pin 'em on your shawl. It's too bad you gotto go. I wisht we could be together for a week. Bet we could find something to talk about every day."

"Mebbe I will come again, in two or three months, but not unless you come first. It's nigh on six months since you darkened my door. Goodbye!"

"Goodbye!" And then a lot of hand waving, as they lost sight of each other.

With rare exceptions, all these women on the backwoods farms were good-hearted old souls. No beggar ever went by their door hungry. Peace to their ashes.

Appendix III
The Quilting Frolic

VASHTA: "Well, folks, here we all be! Less see, there is Pheebe, Betsy, Emily, Ratchel, Marier, Julie and Susan. That makes eight of us and that is just enuff. Six a-sowin, and two to spell, in case someone wants to git a drink of tea or sumthin. If we all sew, and one gits behind, the rest will all hev to wait till that part of the quilt ketches up. Three on a side makes jest nice elbow room, and all gits ready to make a role at the same time. There is some thin pillers there on the longe, if the old quilting frame is too high fer some of ye. If I set it to suit the short ones, the tall ones would hev to bend over, and git the back ake. Hez everybody got a spool of thread? I like that ONT cotton that come round lately. There is a pack of drilled eye needles there in the center. I don't want no more of them punched eye kind. They frazzle the thread, as youl all allow. I think I got it basted good all around, and if you think it aint tite enough, we will pin the roller in another hole."

EMILY: "I see you got that good kind of cotton batten. I wus pullin at the lints and they are nice and long. I had one quilt that went lumpy because the lint was short. A body would hev to quilt it an inch apart to hold it. I like the pattern of your cover. Do you know they are beginning to make quilts out of any shaped pieces of calico, and any color pieces, take em as they run! And they call em crazy quilts, and I low it is a right smart name fer em. I spect some crazy woman made the first one. They say that mebby some day they will make a machine fer doin the quilting. If they do, it won't amount to mutch, fer there aint so mutch of that to do. If they would ony make sumthin that would wash the cloes and the dishes, and keep the house clean, they would be doin sumthin. The trouble is most of the new devilments that comes along takes some pennies away from us. If they would make some masheen that the men folks could sic on the farm work, it would be real handy for the men folks, wouldn't it? Mebby then I could git to York, once in a while, fer the men folks could cook fer themselves then."

PHOEBE: "Well, York is a nice place to go to see things. Mongst other things I onest heard Jenny Lind sing in the old Castle Garden in the Battery, and I hev hardly cared mutch for anyone elses singin since. I wouldn't care to live there stiddy. It is too dangerous, a hull lot of em dies off with the cholera, or small pox every now and then, and it amost burned up twist, the houses is so cluss together that the fire spreads like it would in blue bent grass. The folks that live there stiddy is white and puny lookin. There is too many crowded in together, and anybody knows that too many pigs in a pen won't do well, no matter how mutch you feed em." "I hev been there a good many times on account of sowing pants for Lord and Taylor. But of course I ony stayed there a day or so to look at something and then brung the cloth back with me in a chist, that a stevedore put on the boat fur me. Until later on, I didn't travel that way. One morning, I was waitin for the old boat called the "Columbus" to come in along the North River about acrost the road from where Eben Peek's kill used to be. You've heard of it. That is where the first glazed earthen pie platters, tater bowls and sitch was made in York State. Well, a feller come arunnin over to me and sed "are you goin to York" and I sed yes, and he sed "git right in, it won't cost you nothing. This is the first passenger train to ever go down the Hudson River, and we want to git all the folks on we kin." Peekskill was the end of the line then. Of course, folks travelin now days don't use chists, because they hev trunks now. But they start to throw them off the train long afore it stops, and they up end and bust wide open now and then, and sometimes somme of the wimmins things gits showed up, and everybody laffs. But since Saratoga opened up, they now hev what they call a Saratoga Trunk that is made of sole leather, like what they sole a boot with, and they can't bust them. They cost a hundred dollars, some of them. But the rich folks don't care. Ilebet whats inside gits purty well jumbled up though."

ELIZABETH: "I had some experience with York myself. When I was a girl I went to work there in a 'Hair Seating Factory.' We used to straighten the hair out, and sort sizes, and make nets and what not. They bought hair combings from everywhere, but most of the hair came from Chiney. The coarse hair was used for waterfalls. They had a hoss hair department too. I did not like it there so much and came back to the country and got married. I was always talking about York to my man, and darned if we didn't both go there, and he got to be a "stevedore" (trucking business) and we was doin well. But they were diein off so fast with first one bad disease and another, that we got afraid and came back on a farm. We hev both had a much harder life of it than we had in the city. But we are alive yit, and maybe wouldn't be if we had stayed there."

VASHTA: "I must tell you, Sy says that he don't know wether he made anything by keepin summer boarders or not. There is a lot of young rapscallions that comes along, and about all they think of is tryin to destroy suthin. Most of em is all the time a heavin stuns. One of em have one right through the granery winder. They put chestnut burrs in his linnin duster pockets, and got in the closest somehow and stole most of the steels out of my hoop skirts to make elder snap guns out of. An then shot grains of corn at him with em every time they ketch his back turned. He turned around one time just quick enuf to amost git one in the eye. They leave a lot of dirt out of the fishworm can and a lot of fishworms on the seats of the boat and some dead fish in the bottom for the sun to come out and git at, and then come to him and tell him the boat is astinkin. Ezeff all he hez to do is to clean up after em. He sez it peers like they never seen nothing, and if they git mutch wuss he shant keep em enny more. Asst him what kind of a cow it wus that give the buttermilk, and sitch.

"One of em that was wotchin me skimming the milk sed 'I never knowed there wus so mutch bad stuff that raised into milk that had to be skimmed off and throwed away.' Now that would be a nice thing to do with cream, wouldn't it?

"One of em sed he wanted to see a woodchuck, so one of Sy's hired men that he got to help him git hay told the feller that if he would sneak along slow and peek over the knowll, he might see one on tother side. So he went and peeked over, and shure nuff there wus one out eatin grass. The chucks hole was about half way between him and the boy, and when the chuck seen him, he put fur his hole. The boy seen him acummin and he wheeled around and run rite out from under his hat, and never stopped till he was about out of breth, and half way to the house. When he looked around, he looked clost to his heels to see if the chuck was about to grab him. Of course, the chuck had been in his hole quite a spell by that time. The fellers in the hayfield that could see him from a ways off, liked to busted themselves a laffin. One of em told the boy after that the chuck wouldn't hurt him, and the boy sed 'didn't he run rite at me?' Yes but if you had stood right still, you would hev seen him go in the ground when he got about half way to you. Sy sez that if the fool killers ever start to ketch them all, there is a lot of em in the city that better find a hidin place, as well as them in the country."

RATCHEL: "I allers lowed them city fellers be turr'ble full of old harry. But they are cooped up so that when they git out in the country where there is lots of room they run wild. But they soon git tamed down. After they eat a few green apples, and git a nawful belly ake, they commence to ast then what they hadden dorty eat, and when they stand a hoe or a rake down the wrong way, and then step on it, and the handle flies forward and gives them a lump on the forard the size of a hickory nut, they soond find out how it done it, and when they climb trees and fall lout, they don't genly break anything moren knockin the wind out of em, and they are a little skittish about climin after that. My cousin that married that city feller comes up every summer with her three boys and they do sum damage. They break the cherry tree limbs, and one time left the boat ontied, and it floated over acrost the cove and wore a hole in it on the rocks. I don't think they done it a purpose. But that don't all amount to nothin! We git someone to take care of the house and feed the cattle, and go down and see em around Christmas time. It costs them more to keep us down there, than it does us to keep them up here. They took us to Central Park, to the theatre, and one time to Greenwood Cemetary. We saw Sharlotte Candy's tomb, and it was beautiful. They told me she got killed by a runaway hoss, and her feller was hard hit and as he was wealthy he put up the monument. I disrember what they sed it cost, but it was a nawful lot of money.

"We seen Uncle Toms Cabin one year. The Two Orphans an other, and one time Hyde and Beemans variety show in Brooklyn, and my boy liked that the best. And when we went to the Park it was the monkeys that got most of his attenshin. The last two times they were up, we didn't hev any trouble with them to speak of. But we allers locked the syths, the sickle and the axe in the smoke house, for fear they might get cut, and the saws or the littlest one might be tryin to saw a rock into. Sometimes they would slip up for two or three days in the fall, and we would head them up a nice barrel of large apples. And besides they used to take back Fuzzyvine, Red alder berries on the bush, Bittersweet vines and berries, Creeping pine and colored leaves and ferns that they pressed in a book that they used to fix up their parlor with in the city for Christmas, and although I was used to seein them, the room looked nice, some of the city folks thought it was grand."

MARIER: "I been listening all along, and I don't know when I hev heared so much that I like before. But herein about them three boys put me in mind of three that used to visit me frum that boarding house at the lake. Two of em was pretty wild, but one was quiet, and smart. We used to injoy hearin him speak a piece he called 'Tim Finnigans Wake.' Sometimes we laffed till the teers run down our cheeks. The funniest part was the last, for come to find out Tim want ded a tall! And he raised up and sed 'Bad luck to your dowls, did ye think I was dead?'"

SUSAN: "Say, I wished you folks wouldn't be sayin things to make me laff so. I be behind now, with my part, and you hev made me prick my finger twist. I shall hev to asst someone to spell me, if you don't quit. Lets talk quilt a little. If Vashty had hed three quilts reddy, Ile bet we could almost hev finished em. This second one is most done. One more roll will fetch it."

VASHTA: "The frame is a little in the way of puttin in the little table, jest move it over a couple of feet. I got two quart decanters of cherry corjill, and I put a couple o winks uv new ingland in each one. Your about done, and after we git the old quiltin frame up garret, I will fetch em out. The men folks chaws tobaccur, drinks hard cider, and new ingland rum when they be in the hay field, so I guess we kin snuff and hev our little nip too. I got to go out and tend to the chores. Sy is gone to market today.—Well, here I am back again. Pigs fed, eggs gathered, hay throwed down fur the steers and heffers, and all! I see you are all done and the frame upstairs. Here, try some of this corjill everybody! And come to think of it, Julie has set and quilted put nigh all day and never sed nothing cept mebby to pass the thread, and it is time she tole us sumthin."

JULIE: "There is no use of me tryin to tell you anything about round here. You all know that, and as I hev never been to York, nor kept city boarders, I can't tell you anything that I know myself. But I kin tell you some things my man tole me. He hez been to York quite a few times on bizness. I guess him being supervisor of our town has got something to do with it. Some of them city politishins come up once in a while to hev a gab with him, and he genally goes back with em, and stays a day or two. He tole me they took him up the road (Upper Seventh Ave.) one Sunday where the Vanderbilts and the other ritch folks try out their fast hosses. He sed they stopped in a place they called 'Gabe Cases' and hed a drink or two, and he noticed that most everybody, wimmin and all, was takin a drink they called Tom and Jerry. They put something in a glass, and then took a spoon and put something elses in out of a large bowl, and it looked like a stiff cream colored pudding sauce of some kind. They tole him Yankee Sullivan, the prize fighter used to come there sometimes. But he didn't see him. One time they went to Niblos Garden, and the Crystal Maze. One day his city friends had some private bizness to attend to, and sed he would be gone mebby four hours. So my man went for a walk by hisself. He happened to git in Baxter Street, and they dragged him in to buy a suit of clothes in spite of all the fightin he could do. They almost ripped his coat sleeve clean off at the shoulder arm hole, and he had to go back with it that way to his friends house. When his friend came back, he tole him that he was lucky he didn't git robbed, and that he might hev got lost. Specially if he got down around the five pints. Then he tole him about the feller that went in a three cornered saloon down there that had a three cornered bar. After he had a few drinks, he got a little gabby and they put him out. He went around the corner into what he thought was another saloon. The bartender put him out again, and handled him pretty rough. He said to hisself, I went round the corner to the right, so I will go round to the right again to be shure. So he went around and in again. That time when the bartender put him out he knocked him down. When he got so he could set up on the sidewalk, and look around, he was sober enough to see that it was the same bartender that had put him out three times that stood alookin at him, and he sed to the bartender, 'Do you own all the saloons in New York?' And he tole him about two strange fellers that met on the Bowery, and it happened they both stuttered. One sed to the tother 'Wa-wa-whers Bleeker Street?' And the other one sed 'Ri-ri-right down there,' and the tother one sed 'You-you-you mock me, will ye,' and they went to fightin. Emily, what makes your face so red?"

EMILY: Oh, every time I take a little it goes right to my stummick, nif it would stay there it would be all right, but somehow some of it gits up to my hed. I notice yourn aint so white as it was a while ago, and when I look around, I guess the hull of us is in the same boat."

VASHTA: "You folks act like you would get stewed if you smelt the glass stopper. Here, let me fill em up agin."

EMILY: "No, not me! Well, then, this will be the last."

VASHTA: "Well here is good luck to you all, and I hope we will hev another quilting frolic. Anytime any of you hev one let me know. I thank you for your good work."

SUSAN: "Thash the besh cor-gill I ever drunk!"

ELIZABETH: "Taint the corjill, it's the new ingland, that put the Oh-be-joyful in it."

PHOEBE: "Fi don't look out my man will smell my breth when I get hum."

VASHTA: "Spose he does, slong you kin git supper, that's nigh nuff, ain't it?"

MARIER: "Guess I better be gittin my shawl on to go hum. Its gittin kindy late."

PHOEBE: "I guess we all better be gittin em on."

VASHTA: "You don't want to hurry yourselves off so. Twont be dark in two hours yit."

MARIER: "Now that I am on my feet, my knees seem more limberer than they used to be, and I notice some of the rest of you seem to be steppin up over sumthin that haint there."

ALL EIGHT LADIES: "Purty ni.... who sed.... mebby so.... bet you will.... tohum.... solongs he sed."

SYRUS: "HEH! What in toppet is goin on here? I stopped the hosses bout forty rods frum the house. Thought I heered a flock of wild geese a squankin over, and it wus you wimmin! You must be hevin a lot of fun! Cant ye let me in on it sumhow? I see ye all be fixin to go hum. You needn't hurry off on my count. But if you must go, you kin all pile rite in the old mountin wagin, and ile take you all to hum afore I onhitch the hosses. Only one of ye get in with me so ile hev lots of room to handle the lines. That will make it jest rite. Three apiece in the two hind seats. Be keerful folks gittin in, and don't let your foot slip off that iron step or you will skin your shins off. Julie, give Granny your hand. Now are you all set? Git-Tapp!!"

THE END